PASCAL WITH STYLE

PROGRAMMING PROVERBS

Hayden Computer Programming Series

PASCAL WITH STYLE

HENRY F. LEDGARD
PAUL A. NAGIN
AND
JOHN F. HUERAS

Hayden Book Company

A DIVISION OF HAYDEN PUBLISHING COMPANY, INC.
HASBROUCK HEIGHTS, NEW JERSEY / BERKELEY, CALIFORNIA

Library of Congress Cataloging in Publication Data

Ledgard, Henry F   1943—
    PASCAL with style.

    (Hayden computer programming series)
    Bibliography: p.
    Includes index.
    1. PASCAL (Computer program language)
I. Nagin, Paul A., joint author. II. Heuras, Jon F.,
joint author. III. Title.
QA76.73.P2L4   001.6'424   79-18069
ISBN 0-8104-5124-7

44,011

Printed in the United States of America

		10	11	12	13	14	15	16	17	18	PRINTING
					85	86	87	88	89	90	91	YEAR

FOREWORD

By necessity, computer science, computer education, and computer practice are all embryonic human activities, for they have existed for only a single generation. From the beginning, programming has been a frustrating black art, with individual abilities ranging from the excellent to the ridiculous and often exhibiting very little in the way of systematic mental procedure. In a sense, the teaching of programming through mistakes and debugging can hardly be regarded as legitimate university level course work. At the university level we teach such topics as the notion of an algorithm, concepts in programming languages, compiler design, operating systems, information storage and retrieval, artificial intelligence, and numerical computation; but in order to implement ideas in any of these functional activities, we need to write programs in a specific language.

Students and professionals alike tend to be overly optimistic about their ability to write programs or to make programs work according to preestablished design goals. However, we are beginning to see a breakthrough in programming as a mental process. This breakthrough is based more on considerations of style than on detail. It involves taking style seriously, not only in how programs look when they are completed, but in the very mental processes that create them. In programming, it is not enough to be inventive and ingenious. One also needs to be disciplined and controlled in order not to become entangled in one's own complexities.

In any new area of human activity, it is difficult to foresee latent human capabilities. We have many examples of such capabilities: touch typing, speed writing, and 70-year-old grandmothers who drive down our highways at 70 miles an hour. Back in 1900 it was possible to foresee cars going 70 miles an hour, but the drivers were imagined as daredevils rather than as grandmothers. The moral is that in any new human activity one generation hardly scratches the surface of its capabilities. So it will be in programming as well.

The next generation of programmers will be much more competent than the first one. They will have to be. Just as it was easier to get into college in the "good old days," it was also easier to get by as a programmer in the "good old days." For this new generation, a programmer will need to be capable of a level of precision and productivity never dreamed of before.

This new generation of programmers will need to acquire discipline and control, mainly by learning to write programs correctly from the start. The debugging process will take the new form of verifying that no errors are present, rather than the old form of finding and fixing errors over and over (otherwise known as "acquiring confidence by exhaustion"). Programming is a serious logical business that requires concentration and precision. In this discipline, concentration is highly related to confidence.

In simple illustration, consider a child who knows how to play a perfect game of tic-tac-toe but does not know that he knows. If you ask him to play for something important, like a candy bar, he will say to himself, "I hope I can win." And sometimes he will win, and sometimes not. The only reason he does not always win is that he drops his concentration. He does not realize this fact because he regards winning as a chance event. Consider how different the situation is when the child *knows* that he knows how to play a perfect game of tic-tac-toe. Now he does not say, "I hope I can win." He says instead, "I know I can win; it's up to me!" And he recognizes the necessity for concentration in order to insure that he wins.

In programming, as in tic-tac-toe, it is characteristic that concentration goes hand in hand with justified confidence in one's own ability. It is not enough simply to know how to write programs correctly. The programmer must *know that he knows* how to write programs correctly, and then supply the concentration to match.

This book of proverbs is well suited to getting members of the next generation off to the right start. The elements of style discussed here can help provide the mental discipline to master programming complexity. In essence, the book can help a programmer make a large first step on the road to a new generation of programming.

HARLAN D. MILLS

Federal Systems Division, IBM
Gaithersburg, Maryland

PREFACE

This text was originally motivated by a small book called *Elements of Style*, written by William Strunk, Jr., and revised by E. B. White. Originally conceived in 1918, Strunk's book stressed the need for rigor, conciseness, and clarity in the writing of English prose. In like manner, *PASCAL With Style* is intended for PASCAL programmers who want to write carefully constructed, readable programs.

Many programmers have told us of programming experiences in which a simple set of guidelines could have averted disaster. Although a burned hand may teach a good lesson, we believe that the introduction of well-advised guidelines is an easier and less painful way to achieve good programming. To be sure, rules of style restrict the programmer. However, our hope is to enable the programmer to focus creativity on the deeper issues in programming rather than on problems that obscure the issues.

Several characteristics other than academic ones have been deliberately sought in this book. First, there has been an attempt to be lighthearted. The intention is to encourage a zest for learning that we all need in order to do our more rewarding work. Second, there has been an attempt to be specific. Progress is made when we speak plainly and give examples of what we say.

The programming examples are given in PASCAL, but the points of the examples should be clear even without a detailed knowledge of the PASCAL language. In particular, the programs given here conform to the definition of PASCAL as presented by Jensen and Wirth [J1]* and implemented on the CDC6600.

This book is designed as a guide to better programming, not as an introduction to the details of PASCAL or a similar higher level language. It should be of value to all programmers who have some familiarity with PASCAL. As such, it may be used as a supplementary text in courses where PASCAL programming is a major concern, or as an informal guide to experienced programmers who have an interest in improving software quality. However, we strongly believe that the ideas presented should go hand in hand with learning the PASCAL language itself.

*See the Bibliography at the conclusion of the text for all references.

The reader who dismisses the overall objective of this book with the comment, "I've got to learn all about PASCAL first," may be surprised to find that the study of good programming practices in conjuntion with the basics of the language may reap quick and longstanding rewards.

PASCAL with Style is organized in five major parts. Chapter 1 is an opening statement. Chapter 2 is a collection of simple rules, called *proverbs*. The proverbs summarize in terse form the major ideas of this book. Each proverb is explained and applied. There are a few references to later chapters where various ideas are more fully explored.

Chapter 3 is an introduction to a strict top-down approach for programming problems in any programming language. The approach is oriented toward the easy writing of complete, correct, readable programs. It should be read carefully, because some of its details are critical and not necessarily intuitive. The approach hinges on developing the overall logical structure of the program first.

Chapter 4 gives a set of strict program standards for writing programs. These rules have been strictly followed in this book, and we believe that their adoption is one of the most important factors in achieving quality programs. Chapter 5 elaborates on several important and sometimes controversial ideas discussed in the chapter on programming proverbs.

This effort has been aided by many individuals. Louis Chmura, Andrew Singer, Michael Marcotty, and William Cave deeply influenced our ideas. Louis Chmura, co-author of *COBOL with Style*, also helped to develop many of the ideas and originated the story of Dorothy and Irene. Andrew Singer was the source of a stimulating critique of the whole area of programming and is the best programmer and program designer we have ever met. Michael Marcotty set an example of eloquent programming style and often contributed the right word at the right time. William Cave provided provocative discussions on the writing of large programming systems for day-to-day use.

Edwina Carter, Gail Michael, and Linda Strzegowski provided services without which this book would be but a collection of handwritten pages without a title. William Fastie, Joseph Davison, and Leslie Chaikin were the sources of many ideas taken from the predecessor of this book. Members of the Computer and Information Science Department at the University of Massachusetts provided a solid intellectual environment for this work. We are grateful to all.

PASCAL with Style is surely our own personal statement about programming. Other views have been given by Kernighan and Plauger [Ref. K1], Van Tassel [Ref. V1], and Kreitzberg and Shneidermann [Ref. K2]. Above all else, we firmly believe that the study of guidelines for good programming can be of great value to all programmers and that there are principles that transcend the techniques of any individual practitioner.

HENRY F. LEDGARD
PAUL A. NAGIN
JON F. HUERAS

CONTENTS

PASCAL WITH STYLE

PROGRAMMING
PROVERBS

CHAPTER ONE
THE WAY AHEAD

Things is 'round to help learn programmers, especially them who don't want to pick up no more bad habits, to program good, easy, the first time right, and so somebody else can figger out what they done and why.

For those readers who appreciate diamonds in the rough, the paragraph above represents all that follows.

An indication of the current state of the art of computer programming is that the proud exclamation "It worked the first time!" is rarely heard. Writing programs that work correctly the first time is possible, but unusual. Since programmers undoubtedly try to write programs that work the first time, one wonders why they don't succeed more often. The reasons are simple. First, programming is difficult. Second, there are very few principles for developing and writing good programs. Since few principles exist, each programmer must develop individual ones, often haphazardly.

The reader may well ask, "Why should programs work right the first time?" The reason is not at all obvious. Less compiler time? Less debugging time? Fewer hours at the terminal? Not really. Imagine for the moment that you had to buy one of two computer programs, each 10,000 lines long. Let us not quibble about the cost but assume that the costs are for all purposes equal, about a hundred thousand dollars. Let's even suppose that each program has been thoroughly tested and certified to be absolutely correct. Now imagine that the only other thing you know about the programs is that the first required hundreds of modifications but that the second worked right the first time! Which program would you buy? And *why?*

In reality, the state of the art is considerably worse than the fact that most programs do not work right the first time. Too many programs work only most of the time. Indeed, a few never work at all. What's more, of those that do work correctly, many are laborious to maintain.

There has recently been an increasing concern within the computing community about the quality of software. As a result, a new methodology is emerging, a harbinger of further changes to come. Notable are the works of Mills, Dijkstra, Wirth, Weinberg, Hoare, Wulf, Horning, Parnas, Cave, Strachey, Kosaraju, Knuth, and Marcotty. Many of the developing ideas are useful now. The time has come for programmers to write programs that work correctly the first time. Programs should do the whole job, even if the original problem has been poorly conceived. Programs should be easy to read, understand, and maintain.

For those accustomed to poor program performance, weeks of testing, or long hours deciphering someone else's code, the above statements might seem unrealistic. Nevertheless, there are well-founded principles that can be utilized to achieve these goals. Some of the principles we shall present are obvious, even to novice programmers. Others even experienced programmers might debate. However, before any principle is rejected, it must be remembered that a program is not only a set of descriptions and instructions for a computer, but a *set of descriptions and instructions that must be understood by human beings, especially the one who reads it the most—you, the programmer.*

It is well known that the cost of program development and maintenance today is high and growing. In fact, we have heard it said that the cost of program maintenance on some poorly constructed systems is a hundred times greater than the cost of initial development and testing. To attack these costs, methodology and clarity must be early programming concerns.

In view of today's increasing development and maintenance costs and the decreasing costs of computer hardware it is shortsighted to be overconcerned with various "micro-efficiency" [Ref. A1] techniques that save bytes and milliseconds. The considerations of an "efficient" computer program can no longer ignore overall program costs.

The use of flowcharting as a program development and documentation technique also has been misunderstood and overestimated. A case against program flowcharts is given in Chapter 5. While judicious use of certain types of flowcharts can be a valuable part of the programmer's repertoire, there are numerous other programming techniques that have little need for flowcharts. The reader will observe a scarcity of program flowcharts in this book.

The development of effective algorithms and data structures is an activity that is closely related to general programming techniques. While general programming techniques can offer strong guidelines for the development of a good solution, they will not necessarily help the programmer determine the best data organization scheme, the best numerical algorithm, or the clearest output of results. So advised, we shall proceed to make our case.

CHAPTER TWO
PROGRAMMING PROVERBS

"Experience keeps a dear school, but fools will learn in no other."
Maxim prefixed to *Poor Richard's Almanack*, 1757

Over two centuries ago Ben Franklin published his now familiar *Poor Richard's Almanack*. In it he collected a number of maxims meant as a simple guide to everyday living. Similarly, this chapter is intended as a simple guide to everyday PASCAL programming. As such, it contains a collection of terse statements that serve as a set of practical rules for the PASCAL programmer. These programming proverbs motivate the entire book.

Before going on, a prefatory proverb seems appropriate:

Do Not Break the Rules Before Learning Them

As with most maxims or proverbs the rules are not absolute, but neither are they arbitrary. Behind each one lies a generous nip of thought and experience. We hope the programmer will seriously consider them. At first glance some of them may seem either trivial or too time-consuming to follow. However, we believe that experience will prove the point. Just take a look at past errors, and then reconsider the proverbs.

The programming proverbs, like all old saws, overlook much important detail in favor of easily remembered phrases. Indeed there are some cases where programs should not conform to standard rules; that is, there are exceptions to every proverb. Nevertheless, we think experience will show that these exceptions are rare and that a programmer should not violate the rules without serious reasons.

A list of all the proverbs is given in Table 2.1. It is hard to weigh their relative importance, but they do at least fall into certain categories. The relative importance of one proverb over another depends quite markedly on the programming problem at hand.

Table 2.1   The Programming Proverbs

A Good Start Is Half the Race

1. Don't Panic!
2. Define the Problem Completely.
3. Start the Documentation Early.
4. Think First. Code Later.
5. Proceed Top-Down.
6. Beware of Other Approaches.

Keeping Logical Structure

7. Code in Logical Units.
8. Use Functions and Subroutines.
9. Don't GOTO
10. Prettyprint.

Coding the Program

11. Use Mnemonic Names.
12. Comment Effectively.
13. Make Constants Constant.
14. Get the Syntax Correct Now.
15. Don't Leave the Reader in the Dust.
16. Produce Good Output.
17. Hand-Check the Program.
18. Prepare to Prove the Pudding.

And of Course . . .

19. Have Someone Else Read the Work.
20. Read the Manuals Again.
21. Don't Be Afraid to Start Over!

We close this introduction by noting why we use the word *proverb,* rather than the more accurate word *maxim.* Proverbs and maxims both refer to pithy sayings derived from practical experience. Proverbs are usually well known, whereas maxims are usually not. Admittedly, programming proverbs are not popular sayings. However, the title was chosen with an eye to the future, when hopefully some of these sayings might become true programming proverbs. And, of course, we think that "Programming Proverbs" just sounds better!

Proverb 1   DON'T PANIC

This is the first, but often overlooked, programming proverb. When given a new problem to solve, there are many forces that encourage the programmer to abandon thoughtful and effective programming techniques in favor of quicker, high-pressure, unproven ones. Typically, the programmer may be loaded down with other work. Your instructor or management may be putting on the pressure by setting an unrealistic schedule or by promising a bonus for finishing early. Of course, there is always the natural human tendency to "get on with the job," or in other words, code. Unfortunately, the tendency to try to obtain speedy results is counter to good programming practice.

At the beginning of a programming project, the programmer's good sense must prevail. He or she must develop a thoughtful approach that ensures that the entire programming job is firmly in hand. Not doing so will surely result in a programming environment that is all too common today, where existing code is constantly being reworked as new code shows oversights, bugs hide all over the finished code, and maintenance takes much longer than expected.

If you find yourself upset or ploughing ahead with a new programming assignment,

1. Stop
2. Calm down
3. Return to methodical programming techniques.

We can't emphasize this enough! One of us, in fact, wanted to go further and retitle this proverb "TAKE THE AFTERNOON OFF," but you know what happens to ideas like that.

Proverb 2   DEFINE THE PROBLEM COMPLETELY

Good problem definitions are vital to the construction of good programs. An incomplete or ill-formed definition implies that the complete structure of the problem is not fully understood. Missing information, ignorance of special cases, and an abundance of extraneous information in a definition are good signs of poor programs, or at best, of programs that will be a surprise for the ultimate user. Any program that processes large amounts of data is bound to encounter some simple unnoticed condition, resulting in the all too common program crash.

We have often heard the claim that it is quite permissible to start with an imperfect problem definition, for during later program development a good programmer will readily pick up any critical points missed in the initial definition. We strongly disagree with this view. Starting with solid, complete (albeit laborious) problem definition is often half the solution to the entire problem. Moreover, good definitions can serve as the basis for good program documentation.

There are many reasons why good problem definitions are rare. First, there is no well-accepted idea of what comprises a good definition. Different programmers, instructors, and managers usually employ different definition techniques. For example, some project managers require only program narratives, decision tables, or system flowcharts. Another common practice is to have an experienced system analyst draw up several system flowcharts, some narrative descriptions, and some detailed descriptions of some inputs and outputs. Of course, the quality and completeness of these definitions will vary according to the style of the individual analyst.

Second, there is an almost irresistible temptation to skirt over the issue of definition in order to "get on with the job." This temptation is especially acute when the given problem is similar to previously solved problems or when there is strong external pressure to produce some quick, visible results (that is, programs). Furthermore, even if programmers could avoid the rush to get on with the job, management and the "customer" often make it difficult to invest the time and money in a good problem definition. The results of good definitions often appear to be wasted, since working code is usually delayed, especially when a programmer works hard to ensure that no problem situations go unnoticed.

Third, good problem definitions involve plain hard work. There is an intense amount of persistence and discipline required to get any definition straight.

As an example, consider the definition of Example 2.1a, which defines a program to aid a prospective homeowner in determining the financial arrangements of a mortgage loan. This definition is quite adequate, but on close analysis certain points need to be resolved. The formula that relates the values of the principal, interest rate, number of years, and monthly payment may not be readily available to the programmer. The formats for the input and output are not exactly clear, and several exceptional conditions that can arise in the computation are not mentioned. The definition of Example 2.1b resolves each of the above issues. It is a bit long but far more precise than that of Example 2.1a.

One important point of Example 2.1b is the inclusion of a sample of the input and output. Often a sample printout can be of great value to a programmer in giving a quick synopsis of the problem. In addition, a sample printout can often prevent surprises in cases where the program turns out to be quite different from the expectations of the person defining the problem. If a programmer is not given a sample of the input-output, he or she should try to provide a sample *before* programming.

In Chapter 3 we will discuss several ideas for producing good problem definitions in conjunction with a complete example. However, there are a few points about good definitions that deserve to be mentioned here. First, in attempting to supply a complete problem definition, the programmer probably cannot err by devoting a great deal of time and thought. While perfect definitions are probably unattainable, with good technique and discipline you will end up

Example 2.1 Proposed Definitions of a Mortgage Problem

Example 2.1a   Poor Problem Definition

We wish to devise a program to help potential homeowners assess the finances of mortgaging a home. There are four basic factors to be considered: the principal, the interest rate, the number of years for the mortgage, and the monthly payment. The program must input values for any three of the above quantities, output the fourth quantity, and also output a table indicating how the amount of the first monthly payment of each year is divided between principal and interest.

The input to this program is a line (or card) containing three of the above four figures:

Columns	*Quantity*
1–5	Principal
8–11	Interest rate
14–15	Number of years
18–22	Monthly payment

The principal and number of years are given as integers, the interest rate and monthly payments are given as fixed-point real numbers. The missing quantity is given as zero.

The output is to be a line indicating the value of the missing quantity, and a table giving, for the first monthly payment of each year, the amount contributed to decreasing the principal and the amount paid as interest.

Example 2.1b   Better Problem Definition

(1) *Problem Outline:*   We wish to devise a program to help potential homeowners assess the finances of mortgaging a home. There are four basic quantities to be considered:

P   The principal amount of the mortgage
I   The yearly interest rate for the mortgage
N   The number of years for the duration of the mortgage
M   The constant monthly payment required to pay back the
    principal P over N years at the interest rate I

The above quantities are related by the equation:

$$M = \frac{P * i * (1 + i)^n}{(1 + i)^n - 1}$$

where

$i = I/12 =$ monthly interest rate

$n = 12*N =$ number of monthly periods in N years

Briefly, the program is to input any three of the above quantities, compute and print the fourth quantity, and also print a table specifying how the first monthly payment of each year is divided between interest and principal.

(2) *Input:* The input to this program is a line (or card) of the form

column $\rightarrow$	1	8	14	18
	$\downarrow$	$\downarrow$	$\downarrow$	$\downarrow$
	ddddd	d.dd	dd	ddd.dd
	P	I	N	M

where the d's represent decimal digits such that

P = the principal in dollars
I = the percentage interest rate computed to two decimal places
N = the number of years in interger form
M = the monthly payment in dollars and cents

The value of P, I, N, or M to be computed is given as zero. Except to the right of a decimal point, leading zeros may be replaced by blanks.

(3) *Output:* The output from the program is to consist of two parts:
(a) The value to be computed, using one of the formats:

PRINCIPAL	= \$ddddd
INTEREST RATE	= d.dd
NUMBER OF YEARS	= dd
MONTHLY PAYMENT	= \$ddd.dd

(b) A table giving for the first monthly payment of each year the amount paid to principal and the amount paid to interest. The headings and formats for the table values are as follows:

YEAR	AMT PAID TO PRINCIPAL	AMT PAID TO INTEREST
dd	\$ddd.dd	\$ddd.dd

Except to the right of a decimal point, leading zeros for any value are to be replaced by blanks.

(4) *Exceptional Conditions:* If any of the input values are not in the prescribed format or if any output value is not in the range indicated, the program is to print an appropriate message to the user.

(5) *Sample Input:*

20000	8.00	22	0.00

(6) *Sample Output for Above Input:*

MONTHLY PAYMENT = $154.36

YEAR	AMT PAID TO PRINCIPAL	AMT PAID TO INTEREST
1	21.03	133.33
2	22.77	131.59
.		
.		
.		
25	142.53	11.83

"close" to one. Remember that all languages have rigid rules for the execution of programs, and programmers must be specific to the last detail. If something is left unspecified in the original definition, the programmer will eventually have to face the consequences. At best, the changes that must be made are frustrating and distracting.

Once you believe that a definition is complete, put it aside for a time. Pick it up later, and carefully reread and rethink it. Better still, have someone else read it (see Proverb 19). "Complete" problem definitions have been known to show flaws in the light of a new day. As a final word, make sure that you have a complete *written* description of the problem before you do anything else.

Proverb 3   START THE DOCUMENTATION EARLY

What can we say in one short proverb about a subject that has been discussed, written about, and cursed for years? Many have tried to define, motivate, and analyze good program documentation, the central purpose of which is to provide effective communication of factual information among people. The important thing is to do the documentation early. You will have a close touch with your user's or instructor's requirements; and most important, your understanding of the required program may be greatly enhanced.

On major programming projects, good documentation procedures share several characteristics:

1. *Readability is the chief goal.* Documentation is meant to be read by human beings. With good documentation, the reader does not have to stare at a shelf of material with no idea where to begin. The reader obtains exactly the information required, no more and no less.
2. *Documentation is based on good standards.* The what, when, and how of good documentation are recorded somewhere (i.e., standardized), and help is available to understand the standards.

3. *The required documentation is planned from the beginning.* Some documents are written long before others and serve as guides for the later ones. An efficient secretarial staff and automated aids help manage the load.

4. *Documentation is part of the daily programming process.* Finger-paralyzing treatises on long-forgotten topics are not needed. The documentation system drives the programming process!

5. *The procedures are carefully followed.* There is no pressure to skimp on documentation. Someone asks for needed documentation; someone reads it; and there is reward for producing high-quality documentation.

In all honesty, we must admit to finding few documentation systems as good as all this. It is possible to be involved in a programming project with a less than perfect documentation system. In this event, you should develop your own ideas and procedures early.

We all should be able to recognize good program documentation. The only thing left to do is to begin providing it. While you may not achieve a good documentation system right away, any step in that direction is to be preferred to the confusion that exists. Remember, however, to do it now, not later.

Proverb 4   THINK FIRST, CODE LATER

This proverb is intimately connected with the previous proverbs. After you have settled on the problem definition and its documentation procedures, the essential task is to start thinking about the solution as soon as possible, and to start the actual coding process only after you have devised a clear plan of attack.

Consider carefully the wording of this proverb: *Think first* means *think— do not code!* Start thinking while the problem is fresh in your mind and the deadline is as far away as it will ever be. Consider at least two different ways to solve the problem. Examine the approaches in sufficient detail to discover possible trouble spots or areas where the solution appears difficult. A top-notch program requires a top-notch algorithm.

Code later means *delay coding.* Give yourself some time to weed out difficult parts and polish the algorithm before trying to formalize it in actual code. It is much easier to discard poor thoughts than poor programs.

A common violation of this proverb lies in the approach to programming that we shall call the "linear" approach. In the linear approach, a programmer receives a problem and immediately starts preparing the code to solve it. Avoid this temptation, for it is full of hidden costs and dangers. You will certainly feel foolish continuously revising an ill-conceived program, or in the extreme case, writing a program that already exists on your system.

In conclusion, remember Murphy's second law of programming: It always takes longer to write a program than you think. A corollary might be: The sooner you start coding the program (instead of thinking about it), the longer it will take to finish the job.

Proverb 5   PROCEED TOP-DOWN

A major objective of this book is to advocate the "top-down" approach to programming problems. The top-down approach advocated here is not like conventional methods of programming. Furthermore, the top-down approach is itself subject to several interpretations, some of which overlook important issues. Top-down programming is discussed at length in Chapter 3. The following characteristics of the top-down approach are excerpts from that chapter.

1. *Design in Levels.* The programmer designs the program in *levels,* where a level consists of one or more modules. A module is always "complete," although it may reference unwritten submodules. The first level is a complete "main program." A lower level refines or develops unwritten modules in the upper level. In other words, the modules of a successive level consist of the submodules referenced in the prior level. The programmer may look several levels ahead to determine the best way to design the level at hand.
2. *Initial Language Independence.* The programmer initially uses expressions (often in English) that are relevant to the problem solution, even though the expressions cannot be directly transliterated into code. From statements that are machine and language independent, the programmer moves toward a final machine implementation in a programming language.
3. *Postponement of Details to Lower Levels.* The programmer concentrates on critical broad issues at the initial levels and postpones details (for example, choice of specific algorithms or intermediate data representations) until lower levels.
4. *Formalization of Each Level.* Before proceeding to a lower level, the

Example 2.2   Initial Steps in the Top-Down Approach

P_1 *(First pass)*

initialize program variables

10   get a proposed move

   if   move is legal   *then*
     process the move
     else
     goto 10
   if   the game is not over   *then*
     change players and *goto* 10

end the game and stop

P₁ (Formal)

INITIALIZE (PLAYER,BOARD)
write (INTRODUCTORY—MESSAGES)

repeat

  get (MOVE) from PLAYER

  if LEGAL—MOVE (PLAYER,BOARD,MOVE) *then*
     UPDATE—BOARD (PLAYER,BOARD,MOVE)

     if LEGAL—JUMP (PLAYER,BOARD,MOVE) *and*
     JUMP—CAN—BE—CONTINUED (PLAYER,BOARD,MOVE)
     then
        CONTINUE—THE—JUMP (PLAYER,BOARD,MOVE)

     if NO—KING (BOARD,PLAYER) *and*
     MOVES—LEFT (BOARD,OPPONENT)
     then
        swap PLAYERS
        prompt OPPONENT for next MOVE
    else
        write (WINNING—MSG) for PLAYER
        write (LOSING—MSG) for OPPONENT
        GAME—OVER is TRUE

  else
    write (ILLEGAL—MOVE—MSG) for PLAYER

until GAME—OVER

---

programmer ensures that the "program" in its current stage of development is a "formal" statement. In most cases this means a program that calls unwritten submodules with all arguments spelled out. This step ensures that further sections of the program will be developed independently, without later changing the specifications or the interfaces between modules.

5. *Verification of Each Level.* After generating the modules of a new level, the programmer verifies the developing formal statement of the program.

This ensures that errors pertinent to the current level of development will be detected at their own level.
6. *Successive Refinements.* Each level of the program is refined, formalized, and verified in successive levels until the programmer obtains the completed program that can be transformed easily into PASCAL.

Consider Example 2.2, which gives the first level of the program for the programming problem of Chapter 3. Examining the definition of the problem, the programmer writes a complete but informal main program, P_1. After a somewhat more detailed look at the problem definition and considering the overall algorithm chosen earlier, the programmer develops P_1 into a formal version. The formal main program is in some sense complete and can be verified as if it had been written in an actual programming language. The code to produce the modules referenced in P_1 must be developed in P_2 and further refined in successive levels.

Top-down programming has two distinct advantages. First, a programmer is initially freed from the confines of a particular language and can deal with more natural data structures or actions. Second, it leads to a modular approach that allows the programmer to write statements relevant to the current structures or actions. The details can be developed later in separate modules. In fact, the main goal of top-down programming is just that: to aid the programmer in writing well-structured, modular programs.

We cannot really say it all here! Chapter 3 tells the whole story.

Proverb 6 BEWARE OF OTHER APPROACHES

Traditionally, programmers have used many different approaches to a program. Consider the following list:

1. Bottom-up approach
2. Inside-out or forest approach
3. Linear approach
4. Typical systems analyst approach
5. Imitation approach

In the "bottom-up" approach, the programmer writes the lower modules first and the upper levels later. The bottom-up approach is in a sense the inversion of the top-down approach. It suffers severely by requiring the programmer to make specific decisions about the program before the overall problem and algorithm are understood.

In between the top-down and the bottom-up approaches, we have the "inside-out" or "forest" approach, which consists of starting in the middle of the program and working down and up at the same time. Roughly speaking, it goes as follows:

1. *General Idea.* First we decide upon the general idea for programming the problem.
2. *A Rough Sketch of the Program.* Next we write any "important" sections of the program, assuming initialization in some form. In some sections we write portions of the actual code. In doing this, we hope that the actual intent of each piece of code will not change several times, necessitating rewriting parts of our sketch.
3. *Coding the First Version.* After Step 2, we write specific code for the entire program. We start with the lowest level module. After an individual module has been coded, we debug it and immediately prepare a description of what it does.
4. *Rethinking and Revising.* As a result of Step 3, we should be close to a working program, but it may be possible to improve on it. So we continue by making several improvements until we obtain a complete working program.

We think it fair to say that many programmers often work inside out. Usually they don't start very close to the top or bottom levels. Instead they start in the middle and work outward until a program finally appears on the horizon. The approach is a poor one, for the program may undergo many changes and patches and thus seldom achieves a clear logical structure.

The third method is called the "linear" approach. Here, one immediately starts writing code as it will appear when executed: first line first, second line second, and so forth. The debit with this approach is the need to make specific detailed decisions with very little assurance that they are appropriate to the problem at hand. One must then accept the consequences. This technique may seem obviously poor, but the temptation to use it can be strong, especially on "easy" programs. Beware of this temptation, for there is no such thing as an "easy" program.

The fourth technique is the typical "systems analyst" approach. When used wisely it can be an effective technique, and admittedly it has been successfully used for many large programs. We shall briefly compare it with the top-down approach, the technique advocated in this book.

The systems analyst often starts on a large programming problem by dividing up the task on the basis of the flow of control he sees in the overall program. The flowchart picturing the flow is broken into a number of modules, which are then farmed out to the programmers. After these have been completed, the analyst will firm up the interfaces and try to make things work right. The lower level modules receive attention before their function and data requirements are explicit. The resulting program modules are primarily determined by the flow of control through the program; thus the importance of flowcharts with this technique.

With the top-down approach, on the other hand, the flow of control is subservient to the logical structure. There does not have to be an identifiable flow of control that is easy to flowchart. The flow of control is rather like traversing a tree. It starts at the top level, goes down one or more levels, comes back, goes on to another level, and so forth. The top-down approach thus has little need for flowcharting.

As a final method, consider what we call the "imitation" approach, a method superficially resembling the top-down approach. This approach is discussed in detail because many programmers *think* that the top-down approach is really the way they have always programmed. We claim that there are often subtle but important differences. The imitation approach is described as follows:

1. *Thinking about the Program.* Having been given a programming assignment, take the time to examine the problem thoroughly before starting to program. Think about the details of the program for a while, and then decide on a general approach.
2. *Deciding on Submodules.* After having thought about the problem in detail, decide on what sections will be sufficiently important to merit being made into submodules.
3. *Data Representation.* After compiling a list of the submodules, decide on a data representation that will enable them to be efficient, unless the representation is already specified.
4. *Coding of Submodules.* At this point write each submodule. After each is completed, write down what it expects as input, what it returns as output, and what it does. The submodules should be written in a hierarchical manner: the most primitive first, calling routines second, and so forth. Doing this will ensure that the submodules are fully coded before the upper-level program structures are finalized.
5. *Coding the Main Program.* After all submodules have been written, write the main program. The purpose of the main program will be sequencing and interfacing the subroutines.

The imitation approach has some important resemblances to the top-down approach:

1. The programmer must understand the problem thoroughly before writing code.
2. The actual writing of the program is postponed until after certain decisions have been made.
3. The problem is broken up into logical units.

However, there are important different characteristics in the two approaches.

1. In the top-down approach, a *specific* plan of attack is developed in stages. Only the issues relevant to a given level are considered, and these issues are formalized completely.

2. Furthermore, whenever the programmer decides to use a subprogram or procedure, the interfaces (i.e., arguments, returned values, and effects) are decided *first*. The inputs and outputs are formalized before developing the submodule; that is, the submodules are made to fit the calling routine instead of the other way around.

3. Most important, at *every step* in the top-down approach, the programmer must have a complete, correct "program."

The major disadvantages of the imitation approach are that it is more likely to produce errors, to require major program modifications, or to result in a somewhat ill-conceived program. Choosing a partially specified attack may require serious changes to the program. Coding submodules first may result in a confusing program logic if the submodules do not happen to integrate easily into the upper level code designed later.

In summary, think carefully about programming technique. The top-down approach, which is discussed at length in Chapter 3, may provide a wise alternative.

Proverb 7 CODE IN LOGICAL UNITS

The best programs are those that can be understood easily. There are no superfluous details and the logical structure is clear. Such well-structured programs are always a by-product of a careful development process and are usually characterized by small, functionally specific modules. Generally, the statements of a PASCAL module should not extend beyond one page.

The most direct value of modular code is felt during program maintenance, for time is not wasted trying to determine what is being done over several sections of code. Consider Fig. 2.1a which outlines the logical structure of a hypothetical program. The structure is difficult to follow. Figure 2.1b pictures the remedied situation where simple computations are isolated in units.

There are many assets to modular code. Coding time is shortened by the use of previously written modules. Implementation costs are lower because of easier overlaying, decreased recompilation costs, smaller tasks, and isolated code bottlenecks. Testing is much simpler because of the fact that "simple" modules usually have no more than, say, a half dozen looping and branching constructs and thus a small number of total execution paths.

When the time comes to write actual code, there are three guidelines that will help you code in logical units:

1. First and most obviously, make good use of functions and procedures.
2. Avoid confusing control structures.
3. Display the resulting logical structure with good spacing and indentation.

The next three proverbs treat these issues.

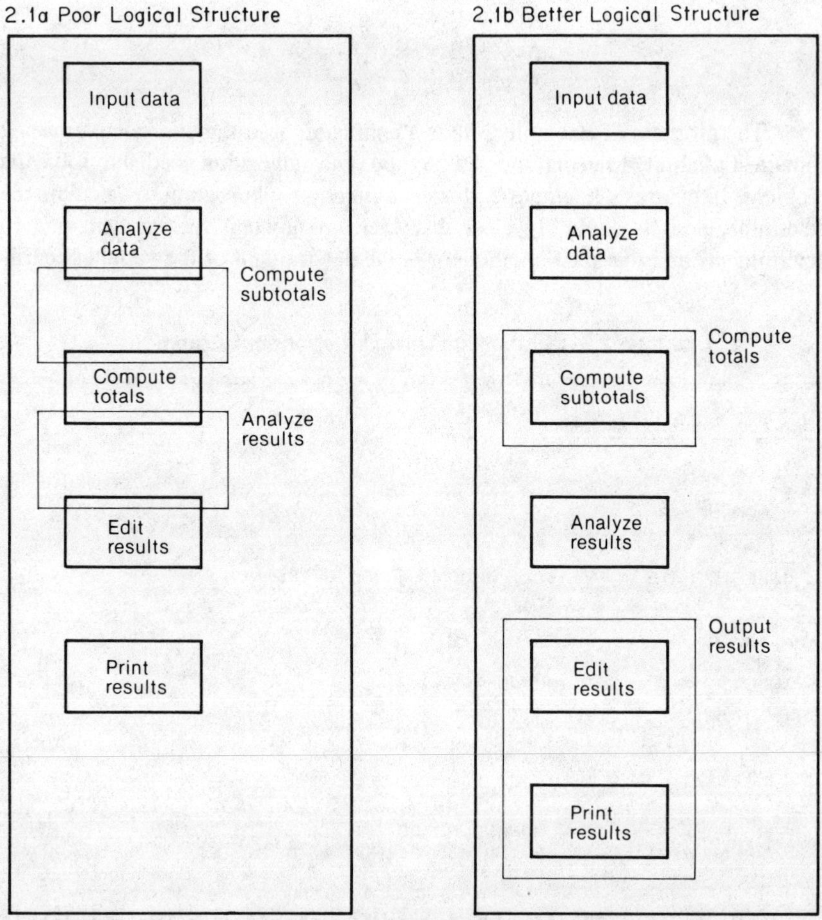

2.1a Poor Logical Structure

Input data

Analyze
data

Compute
subtotals

Compute
totals

Analyze
results

Edit
results

Print
results

2.1b Better Logical Structure

Input data

Analyze
data

Compute
totals

Compute
subtotals

Analyze
results

Output
results

Edit
results

Print
results

Fig. 2.1   Display of logical structure

Proverb 8   FUNCTIONS AND PROCEDURES

The function and procedure facilities in PASCAL can be powerful tools for coding clear, modular programs. Not only do these facilities allow the programmer to "factor out" frequently executed sections of code, but more important, they provide a basic unit for abstraction of program modules. This abstraction can have a great effect on program readability by exposing the program's logical structure, *even if* the function or procedure is called only once.

Consider the programs of Example 2.3. Given the values for the three-element arrays A, B, C, and D, the programs use the determinant method (assuming DENOM is nonzero) to solve three independent equations of the following form for the unknowns x, y, and z:

$$A_1x + B_1y + C_1z = D_1$$
$$A_2x + B_2y + C_2z = D_2$$
$$A_3x + B_3y + C_3z = D_3$$

The program of Example 2.3a is a confusion of arithmetic calculations. It contains little hint of the determinant method or the algorithm needed to solve the problem. In contrast, Example 2.3b uses a function subprogram to calculate the determinants. It is explicitly clear that each unknown is the quotient of two determinants and that the denominator is the determinant of the variable coeffi-

Example 2.3 Solution of Three Independent Equations

2.3a   Poor Solution: Functions Not Used

```
CONST
   NUMUNKNOWNS = 3;

TYPE
   COEFFICIENTS = ARRAY[1..NUMUNKNOWNS] OF REAL;

VAR
   A, B, C, D    : COEFFICIENTS;
   DENOM, X, Y, Z: REAL;
   INDEX         : 1..NUMUNKNOWNS;


BEGIN

   FOR INDEX := 1 TO NUMUNKNOWNS DO
      READLN(A[INDEX], B[INDEX], C[INDEX], D[INDEX])


   DENOM :=  (A[1]*B[2]*C[3]) + (A[2]*B[3]*C[1]) + (A[3]*B[1]*C[2])
            -(A[3]*B[2]*C[1]) - (A[2]*B[1]*C[3]) - (A[1]*B[3]*C[2]);


   X     :=  (D[1]*B[2]*C[3]) + (D[2]*B[3]*C[1]) + (D[3]*B[1]*C[2])
            -(D[3]*B[2]*C[1]) - (D[2]*B[1]*C[3]) - (D[1]*B[3]*C[2]);

   Y     :=  (A[1]*D[2]*C[3]) + (A[2]*D[3]*C[1]) + (A[3]*D[1]*C[2])
            -(A[3]*B[2]*C[1]) - (A[2]*D[1]*C[3]) - (A[1]*D[3]*C[2]);

   Z     :=  (A[1]*B[2]*D[3]) + (A[2]*B[3]*D[1]) + (A[3]*B[1]*D[2])
            -(A[3]*B[2]*D[1]) - (A[2]*B[1]*D[3]) - (A[1]*B[3]*D[2]);

   X     := X / DENOM;
   Y     := Y / DENOM;
   Z     := Z / DENOM;

   WRITELN(X, Y, Z)


END
```

2.3b   Better Solution: A Function Used

```
CONST
   NUMUNKNOWNS = 3;

TYPE
   COEFFICIENTS = ARRAY[1..NUMUNKNOWNS] OF REAL;

VAR
   A, B, C, D      : COEFFICIENTS;
   DENOM, X, Y, Z: REAL;
   INDEX           : 1..NUMUNKNOWNS;


FUNCTION DETERM(X1,X2,X3, Y1,Y2,Y3, Z1,Z2,Z3: REAL): REAL;

BEGIN

   DETERM :=  (X1*Y2*Z3) + (X2*Y3*Z1) + (X3*Y1*Z2)
             -(X3*Y2*Z1) - (X2*Y1*Z3) - (X1*Y3*Z2)

END; (* DETERM *)


BEGIN

   FOR INDEX := 1 TO NUMUNKNOWNS DO
      READLN(A[INDEX], B[INDEX], C[INDEX], D[INDEX])


   DENOM := DETERM(A[1],B[1],C[1], A[2],B[2],C[2], A[3],B[3],C[3]);

   X     := DETERM(D[1],B[1],C[1], D[2],B[2],C[2], D[3],B[3],C[3]);
   Y     := DETERM(A[1],D[1],C[1], A[2],D[2],C[2], A[3],D[3],C[3]);
   Z     := DETERM(A[1],B[1],D[1], A[2],B[2],D[2], A[3],B[3],D[3]);

   X     := X / DENOM;
   Y     := Y / DENOM;
   Z     := Z / DENOM;


   WRITELN(X, Y, Z)

END
```

2.3c   Still Better Solution: Using a Function and Passing Arrays

```
CONST
   NUMUNKNOWNS = 3;

TYPE
   COEFFICIENTS = ARRAY[1..NUMUNKNOWNS] OF REAL;

VAR
   A, B, C, D      : COEFFICIENTS;
   DENOM, X, Y, Z: REAL;
   INDEX           : 1..NUMUNKNOWNS;
```

```
FUNCTION DETERM(R, S, T: COEFFICIENTS): REAL;

BEGIN

   DETERM := (R[1]*S[2]*T[3]) + (R[2]*S[3]*T[1]) + (R[3]*S[1]*T[2])
            -(R[3]*S[2]*T[1]) - (R[2]*S[1]*T[3]) - (R[1]*S[3]*T[2])

END; (* DETERM *)


BEGIN

   FOR INDEX := 1 TO NUMUNKNOWNS DO
      READLN(A[INDEX], B[INDEX], C[INDEX], D[INDEX])

   DENOM := DETERM(A, B, C);

   X    := DETERM(D, B, C) / DENOM;
   Y    := DETERM(A, D, C) / DENOM;
   Z    := DETERM(A, B, D) / DENOM;


   WRITELN(X, Y, Z)

END
```

cient matrix. Example 2.3c shows an even greater improvement when the arrays are passed as arguments.

In brief, use functions and procedures *often*. Even if your program is longer as a result, they can make it more structured and easier to understand.

Proverb 9 DON'T GOTO

Over the past ten years, one programming issue has been the subject of more papers, more opinions, and more controversy than any other: control structures. The control structures for specifying the flow of control in a program are indeed important. At every point in a program the next action to be carried out must be specified. In many languages, the control structure issue focuses on one small statement—the GOTO.

The unconditional transfer of control, which is the function of the GOTO statement, has been associated with programming since its inception. Its historical ties have left indelible marks on today's major programming languages. Until recently, virtually all higher level languages have had some form of an unrestricted GOTO. Yet, of all the linguistic constructs in today's languages, few have been debated more often or more intensively. The GOTO is not intrinsically evil, but its abuses can be avoided by using more transparent linguistic features and by using the GOTO in a highly controlled manner.

Example 2.4   Elimination of GOTOs in Favor of FOR-Loops

2.4a   Poor

```
CONST
   MAXINT = 100;

VAR
   SUM, COUNT: REAL;

LABEL
   10, 20;


BEGIN


   SUM   := 0;
   COUNT := 0;

10: IF COUNT > MAXINT THEN
       GOTO 20;

   SUM   := SUM + COUNT;
   COUNT := COUNT + 1;

   GOTO 10;

20: WRITELN('SUM = ', SUM)


END
```

2.4b   Better

```
CONST
   MAXINT = 100;

VAR
   SUM, COUNT: REAL;

BEGIN

   SUM := 0;

   FOR COUNT := 1 TO MAXINT DO
       SUM := SUM + COUNT;

   WRITELN('SUM = ', SUM)


END
```

Example 2.5 Elimination of GOTOs in Favor of IF Statements and Built-In Functions

---

2.5a   Poor

```
    IF A > B THEN
        GOTO 10;

    D := B - A;

    GOTO 20;

10: D := A - B;

20: WRITELN(D);
```

2.5b   Better

```
    D := A - B;

    IF D < O THEN
        D := -D;

    WRITELN(D);
```

2.5c   Best

```
    D := ABS(A-B);

    WRITELN(D);
```

The fundamental position of the authors is to permit only those control structures for which the programmer can develop a "static" assessment of a program or program fragment. Chapter 4 gives a list of the control structures that we believe are sufficient for wisely handling the control structure problem in PASCAL. For the rest of this proverb, we will concentrate on the major culprit, the GOTO.

Consider first the very simple Examples 2.4 and 2.5, and notice the elimination of GOTOs in favor of FOR loops, IF statements, and built-in functions. With their removal, a clearer structure arises, and the program shortens.

In a more realistic setting, consider the two programs of Example 2.6. Here we see simple subroutines for finding an occurrence of a substring (designated by two character positions) in a given target string. Under certain conditions, the subroutine sets an error flag. In Example 2.6a, we see a quite tightly nested series of interconnected IF statements. The next example, 2.6b, is a program derived from the use of alternative control structures. The second example provides a much clearer description of the algorithm, mainly beause of the use of simple 1-in, 1-out control structures.

The differences between these two programs are quite clearly expressed in their corresponding flowcharts, shown in Figs. 2.2 and 2.3. In the first illustration, the flowchart shows a profusion of branching lines; in the second, a clearer structure is evident.

In another setting, consider the program segments of Example 2.7. These segments employ a variation of the bubble sort algorithm to sort an array A, containing 500 entries. The subroutine SWAP exchanges the values of the two variables given as arguments. Basically, the programs scan the array A once from the top (position 1) to the bottom (position 500). At each examined position in the array, the elements at the top of the position are already in order, and the program checks to see if the element in the next position is itself in order. If not, the element is swapped with the previous element and then "bubbled" up until its proper place in the sorted part of the array is found. Processing then continues at the position below the element originally examined.

Example 2.6 Control Structures

2.6a Poor

```
CONST
   MAXSTRLENGTH = 80;

TYPE
   STRING = ARRAY[1..MAXSTRLENGTH] OF CHAR;

PROCEDURE EXTRACT( (* FROM       *) SOURCESTR          : STRING;
                   (* OF LENGTH  *) STRLENGTH          : INTEGER;
                   (* POSITIONS  *) BEGINPOS, ENDPOS:    INTEGER;
                   (* RETURNING  *) VAR SUBSTR         : STRING;
                   (* OF LENGTH  *) VAR SUBSTRLENGTH:    INTEGER;
                   (* UNLESS     *) VAR ERROR          : BOOLEAN);

VAR
   STRINDEX, SUBSTRINDEX: INTEGER;

LABEL
   10, 15, 20, 25, 30, 40;
```

```
BEGIN

    IF (BEGINPOS - 1) < 0
        THEN
            GOTO 10
        ELSE
            GOTO 15;

10: ERROR := TRUE;
    GOTO 40;

15: IF (ENDPOS - 1) < 0
        THEN
            GOTO 10
        ELSE
            GOTO 20;

20: SUBSTRLENGTH := (ENDPOS - BEGINPOS) + 1;

    IF (STRLENGTH - SUBSTRLENGTH) < 0
        THEN
            GOTO 10
        ELSE
          GOTO 25;

25: IF (MAXSTRLENGTH - SUBSTRLENGTH) < 0
        THEN
            GOTO 10
        ELSE
            GOTO 30;


30: ERROR := FALSE;

    FOR STRINDEX := BEGINPOS TO ENDPOS DO
        BEGIN
            SUBSTRINDEX := (STRINDEX - BEGINPOS) + 1;
            SUBSTR[SUBSTRINDEX] := SOURCESTR[STRINDEX]
        END;

40: (* RETURN *)


END; (* EXTRACT *)
```

2.6b Better

```
CONST
   MAXSTRLENGTH = 80;

TYPE
   STRING = ARRAY[1..MAXSTRLENGTH] OF CHAR;

PROCEDURE EXTRACT( (* FROM      *) SOURCESTR         : STRING;
                   (* OF LENGTH *) STRLENGTH         : INTEGER;
                   (* POSITIONS *) BEGINPOS, ENDPOS: INTEGER;
                   (* RETURNING *) VAR  SUBSTR       : STRING;
                   (* OF LENGTH *) VAR SUBSTRLENGTH: INTEGER;
                   (* UNLESS    *) VAR ERROR         : BOOLEAN);
```

```
VAR
   STRINDEX, SUBSTRINDEX: INTEGER;

BEGIN

   IF (BEGINPOS <= 0) OR (ENDPOS <= 0)
      THEN
         ERROR := TRUE

      ELSE
         BEGIN

            SUBSTRLENGTH := (ENDPOS - BEGINPOS) + 1;

            IF (SUBSTRLENGTH > STRLENGTH) OR (SUBSTRLENGTH > MAXSTRLENGT
               THEN
                  ERROR := TRUE

               ELSE
                  BEGIN

                     ERROR := FALSE;

                     FOR STRINDEX := BEGINPOS TO ENDPOS DO
                        BEGIN
                           SUBSTRINDEX := (STRINDEX - BEGINPOS) + 1;
                           SUBSTR[SUBSTRINDEX] := SOURCESTR[STRINDEX]
                        END

                  END

         END

END; (* EXTRACT *)
```

Example 2.7 A Variant of the Bubble Sort Algorithm

2.7a Poor

```
CONST
   NUMELEMENTS = 500;

VAR
   I, J : INTEGER;
   A    : ARRAY[1..NUMELEMENTS] OF REAL;

LABEL
   10, 20, 30, 40, 50;


BEGIN

   I := NUMELEMENTS;

10: IF I = 1 THEN
      GOTO 50;

   J := 1;
```

```
20:  IF  J = I  THEN
          GOTO 40;

     IF  A[J] <= A[J+1]  THEN
          GOTO 30;

     SWAP  (A[J], A[J+1];

30:  J := J + 1;
     GOTO 20,

40:  I := I - 1;
     GOTO 10;

50:  FOR I := 1 TO NUMELEMENTS DO
          WRITELN(A[I])


END
```

2.7b   Better

```
CONST
    NUMELEMENTS = 500;

VAR
    I, J :  INTEGER;
    A    :  ARRAY[1..NUMELEMENTS] OF REAL;


BEGIN

    FOR I := NUMELEMENTS DOWNTO 2 DO

        FOR J := 1 TO (I-1) DO

            IF  A[J] > A[J+1]
                THEN
                    SWAP  (A[J], A[J+1]);


        FOR I := 1 TO NUMELEMENTS DO
            WRITELN(A[I])

END
```

The PASCAL program of Example 2.7a is oriented towards the efficient use of the GOTO statement. The resulting program is somewhat difficult to understand. The program of Example 2.7b avoids the use of GOTO altogether.

One major point of this example is that the (possibly) small gain in efficiency via the GOTO is not as important as the improvement in clarity when the programmer uses alternative ways of constructing his program.

In summary, the deeper issue here is not merely the elimination of GOTOs but the use of a clear, logical program structure. The trouble with GOTOs is that

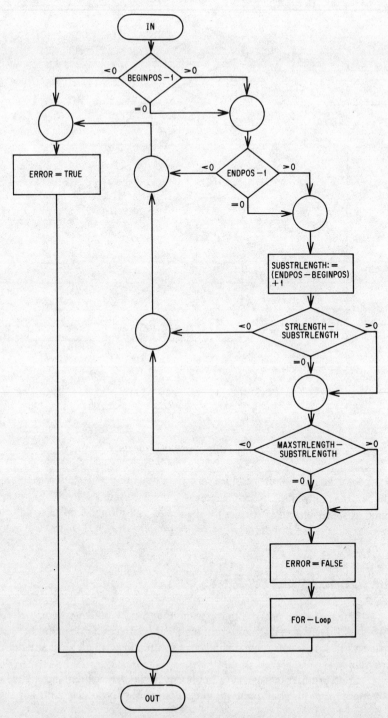

Fig. 2.2   Flowchart for Example 2.6a

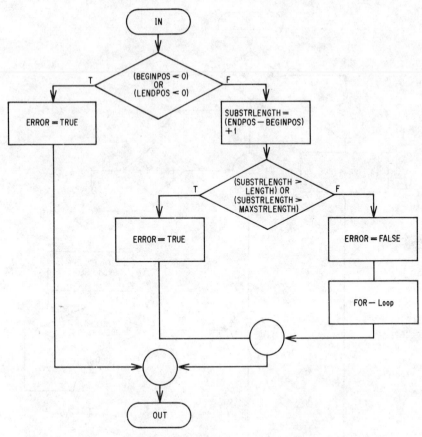

Fig. 2.3   Flowchart for Example 2.6b

when they are abused, they can lead a programmer down the path of a confusing, almost spaghetti-like, logic. Chapter 4, which discusses PASCAL program standards, provides specific rules for the use of well-formed control structures. If you stick to these standards *from the beginning*, the GOTO problem may go away.

Proverb 10   PRETTYPRINT

If there is one proverb that is simple to follow but enormously effective, this is it. Briefly stated, "prettyprinting" is the effective utilization of "extra" spaces, blank lines, or special characters to illuminate the logical structure of a program.

Prettyprinting is especially important in the verification and maintenance of programs. With good prettyprinting it is fairly easy to detect errors, such as improperly structured data description entries and incorrectly nested IF statements. Furthermore, a programmer trying to read the program does not have to devote extra time to discovering its structure, an advantage that makes it considerably easier to understand.

The PASCAL language allows a generous use of blank spaces and lines to promote prettyprinting. As an example, two complete PASCAL programs are listed in Examples 2.8a and 2.8b. The first is not well prettyprinted; the second shows careful thought in prettyprinting. Even in some textbooks, users of PASCAL are seldom exposed to the full possibilities of prettyprinting, although almost every implementation admits great latitude in the spacing of programs.

There is one especially important point—the use of blank lines. The blank line is excellent for separating modules of the program and highlighting critical sections. Examine prettyprinted Example 2.8b. Note how logical sections of the program become apparent solely because of the use of blank lines.

In all our examples, we have attempted to incorporate certain prettyprinting standards. Appendix B itemizes most of these standards; they are the product of many revisions and should be useful to all PASCAL programmers. We encourage the reader to make use of additional prettyprinting standards as

Example 2.8 Prettyprinting

2.8a   Giving Token Thought to Prettyprinting

```
VAR
    CHARACTER: CHAR;
    ACOUNT, ECOUNT, ICOUNT, OCOUNT, UCOUNT: INTEGER;

BEGIN

    ACOUNT:=0;
    ECOUNT:=0;
    ICOUNT:=0;
    OCOUNT:=0;
    UCOUNT:=0;

    WHILE NOT EOF DO BEGIN
    READLN(CHARACTER);
    IF CHARACTER IN ['A','E','I','O','U'] THEN
        CASE CHARACTER OF
            'A': ACOUNT  : = ACOUNT+1;
            'E': ECOUNT  : = ECOUNT+1;
            'I': ICOUNT  : = ICOUNT+1;
            'O': OCOUNT  : = OCOUNT+1;
            'U': UCOUNT  : = UCOUNT+1
        END
    END;

    WRITELN('A=',ACOUNT,'E=',ECOUNT,'I=',ICOUNT,'O=',OCOUNT,
            'U=',UCOUNT)

END
```

2.8b Good Prettyprinting

```
VAR
    CHARACTER: CHAR;

    ACOUNT,
    ECOUNT,
    ICOUNT,
    OCOUNT,
    UCOUNT:   INTEGER;

BEGIN

    ACOUNT := 0;
    ECOUNT := 0;
    ICOUNT := 0;
    OCOUNT := 0;
    UCOUNT := 0;

    WHILE NOT EOF DO
        BEGIN

            READLN(CHARACTER);

            IF CHARACTER IN ['A', 'E', 'I', 'O', 'U'] THEN

                CASE CHARACTER OF

                    'A':  ACOUNT := ACOUNT + 1;

                    'E':  ECOUNT := ECOUNT + 1;

                    'I':  ICOUNT := ICOUNT + 1;

                    'O':  OCOUNT := OCOUNT + 1;

                    'U':  UCOUNT := UCOUNT + 1

                END; (* CASE *)

        END; (* WHILE *)

    WRITELN( 'A = ', ACOUNT,
             'E = ', ECOUNT,
             'I = ', ICOUNT,
             'O = ', OCOUNT,
             'U = ', UCOUNT)

END
```

they are discovered. But do not hesitate to use the standards as they appear. If the program you are writing has a good logical structure, then show it!

Proverb 11   USE MNEMONIC NAMES

It is difficult to overestimate the value of using good, mnemonic, user-defined names. It is all too easy to become careless and use names that may later complicate or confuse the intent of a program. Principles for selecting good mnemonic names are discussed at length in Chapter 5. Here it is sufficient to make one point: Use names that correctly reflect the objects they are intended to represent.

The disadvantage of poor names is easily seen in Example 2.9. The programmer who writes code like the one shown in Example 2.9a will probably need to keep a separate list specifying what each variable name represents. Otherwise the programmer may lose track of what each variable does. Example 2.9b significantly clarifies the situation. The names themselves almost state the intended calculation.

Example 2.9b, however, is written using variable names with a maximum length of six characters (the requirement in standard FORTRAN). Example 2.9c shows the possibilities in PASCAL, and Example 2.9d illustrates the possibilities in languages like PL/1 that allow break characters within names. Certainly OVERTIMEWAGE and OVERTIME__WAGE are more informative than OVTIME.

Example 2.9 Use of Mnemonic Names

2.9a Poor (BASIC Revisited)

```
LET G = (W * H) + (O * X)
LET T = R1 * G
LET S = S1 * G
LET P = G - T - S
```

2.9b Better (FORTRAN Revisited)

```
GROSS = (WAGE * HOURS) + (OVTIME * XHOURS)
TAX   = TXRATE * GROSS
SSEC  = SSRATE * GROSS
PAY   = GROSS - TAX - SSEC
```

2.9c Best (Good Use of PASCAL)

```
GROSSPAY     = (WAGE * HOURS) + (OVERTIMEWAGE * EXTRAHOURS);
TAX          = TAXRATE * GROSSPAY;
SOCSECURITY  = SOCSECRATE * GROSSPAY;
NETPAY       = GROSSPAY - TAX - SOCSECURITY;
```

2.9d The PL/1 Option

```
GROSS_PAY    = (WAGE * HOURS) + (OVERTIME_WAGE * EXTRA_HOURS);
TAX          = TAX_RATE * GROSS_PAY;
SOC_SECURITY = SOC_SEC_RATE * GROSS_PAY;
NET_PAY      = GROSS_PAY - TAX - SOC_SECURITY;
```

The major reason for using good mnemonic names is to improve readability. It is worth the extra time to devise and use informative names. A programmer may not fully appreciate their value until a large program has to be debugged or modified months later. The mnemonic assistance is then priceless.

Proverb 12   COMMENT EFFECTIVELY

Comments are a form of internal documentation that allows the programmer to describe the internal workings of a program. One example will suffice to make the point. Consider the program of Example 2.10a. This program represents the ultimate in obscurity, a program with no comments. The reader is invited to examine the program and determine the meaning of each statement.

Next consider the program of Example 2.10b. The comments convey the logical structure of the program. This information is particularly valuable to someone who is using the program without a copy of the documentation or to someone who doesn't want to spend any excess time trying to figure out the program.

The comments in Example 2.10b, however, are not optimal. Example 2.10c shows a deeper concern for the reader. The comments are clearly separated from the code and give more precise statements about the entire function, even telling us about Euclid's algorithms.

Although the value of using comments can be illustrated over and over again, the programmer is often tempted not to use them. After all, when a programmer is writing a piece of code, comments may not be needed. But how many times during coding does the programmer go back to try to figure out what has happened and what is left to do? And what about the next day? Or the next week? Or the occasion when you are asked to change someone else's program?

One additional proverb is useful here: *Temperance is moderation in all things*. Comments can be overused as well as misused. It is far better to use good prettyprinting and good mnemonic names rather than to clutter up your code with copious comments. Comments should convey useful information. Frequent comments like

$$(* \qquad ** \text{ A GETS B PLUS C} \qquad *)$$
$$A := B + C;$$

not only clutter up your program but may completely discourage anyone from trying to wade through it. In short, comments can promote the design of truly maintainable programs. They can really make a difference. *Use them, temperately*.

Example 2.10 Use of Effective Comments

2.10a   Poor Solution: No Comments

```
FUNCTION GCD(FIRSTNUM, SECONDNUM: INTEGER): INTEGER;

VAR
   HIVALUE, LOVALUE, REMAINDER: INTEGER;

BEGIN

   HIVALUE := MAX(FIRSTNUM, SECONDNUM);
   LOVALUE := MIN(FIRSTNUM, SECONDNUM);

   REPEAT

      REMAINDER := HIVALUE MOD LOVALUE;

      HIVALUE := LOVALUE;
      LOVALUE := REMAINDER

   UNTIL REMAINDER = 0;

   GCD := HIVALUE

END; (* GCD *)
```

2.10b   Better Solution: Paying Token Regard to Good Commenting

```
(*
*    ** FUNCTION TO COMPUTE THE GREATEST COMMON DIVISOR
*    ** OF TWO NUMBERS USING EUCLID'S ALGORITHM.
*)

FUNCTION GCD(FIRSTNUM, SECONDNUM: INTEGER): INTEGER;

VAR
   HIVALUE, LOVALUE, REMAINDER: INTEGER;

BEGIN

   HIVALUE := MAX(FIRSTNUM, SECONDNUM);
   LOVALUE := MIN(FIRSTNUM, SECONDNUM);

   (* PEFORM EUCLID'S ALGORITHM UNTIL GCD IS FOUND *)
```

```
   REPEAT

      REMAINDER : = HIVALUE MOD LOVALUE;

      HIVALUE : = LOVALUE;
      LOVALUE : = REMAINDER

   UNTIL REMAINDER = 0;


   GCD : = HIVALUE


END; (* GCD *)
```

2.10c Best Solution: Careful Commenting

```
(*
*    **   ABSTRACT -
*    **      USE EUCLID'S ALGORITHM FOR COMPUTING THE GREATEST COMMON
*    **   DIVISOR OF TWO INTEGERS:
*    **
*    **   (1)   THE REMAINDER AFTER DIVISION OF THE LARGER BY THE
*    **         SMALLER OF THE TWO NUMBES IS COMPUTED.
*    **
*    **   (2)   IF NONZERO, IT BECOMES THE NEXT DIVISOR, WHILE THE
*    **         ORIGINAL DIVISOR BECOMES THE NEXT DIVIDEND.
*    **
*    **   (3)   THE PROCESS REPEATS UNTIL THE REMAINDER EQUALS ZERO;
*    **         THE CURRENT DIVISOR IS THEN RETURNED AS THE GCD.
*)

FUNCTION GCD(FIRSTNUM, SECONDNUM: INTEGER): INTEGER;


VAR
   HIVALUE, LOVALUE, REMAINDER: INTEGER;


BEGIN

   HIVALUE : = MAX (FIRSTNUM, SECONDNUM);
   LOVALUE : = MIN (FIRSTNUM, SECONDNUM);


   REPEAT

      REMAINDER : = HIVALUE MOD LOVALUE;

      HIVALUE : = LOVALUE;
      LOVALUE : = REMAINDER

   UNTIL REMAINDER = 0;


   GCD : = HIVALUE


END; (* GCD *)
```

Proverb 13   MAKE CONSTANTS CONSTANT

The result of this proverb is most valuable after a program is written, in other words, during program testing or maintenance. The essential idea is to make sure that all constant data items are recognized and given a value in a constant declaration. Furthermore, no executable statement should modify these constant data items.

Consider the programming situation of Example 2.11a. The programmer assumed that the table would always contain 50 elements. The integer 50, besides its use in constructing tables, was used freely throughout the programs in computing averages and controlling conditions. When an increase in data items resulted in 100 elements, changing the number 50 to 100 was a searching chore, for it was all too easy to miss an occurrence of the integer 50. This is not the case with Example 2.11b, where a data name was created and given a value in the constant declaration.

Example 2.11   Integer Constants

2.11a   Poor

```
VAR
    AVERAGE, TOTAL: REAL;
    INDEX         : INTEGER;
    LIST          : ARRAY[1..50] OF REAL;


BEGIN

        .
        .
        .

    TOTAL := 0;

    FOR INDEX := 1 TO 50 DO
        TOTAL := TOTAL + LIST[INDEX];

    AVERAGE := TOTAL / 50;

        .
        .
        .

    FOR INDEX := 1 TO 50 DO
        WRITELN(LIST[INDEX]);

    WRITELN('AVERAGE VALUE = ', AVERAGE);

        .
        .
        .

END
```

2.11b   Better

```
CONST
   NUMELEMENTS = 50;

VAR
   AVERAGE, TOTAL: REAL;
   INDEX         : INTEGER;
   LIST          : ARRAY[1..NUMELEMENTS] OF REAL;

BEGIN

       .
       .
       .

   TOTAL := 0;

   FOR INDEX := 1 TO NUMELEMENTS DO
      TOTAL := TOTAL + LIST[INDEX];

   AVERAGE := TOTAL / NUMELEMENTS;

       .
       .

   FOR INDEX := 1 TO NUMELEMENTS DO
      WRITELN(LIST[INDEX]);

   WRITELN('AVERAGE VALUE = ', AVERAGE);

       .
       .

END
```

A similar issue occurs with real numbers, even if they remain constant. Consider the simple code fragments of Example 2.12. Even the simple conversion factor of Example 2.12b is clearer when given a name.

Example 2.12 Real Constants

2.12a   Poor

```
FUNCTION CENTIGRADE(FARENHEIT: REAL): REAL;
BEGIN

   CENTIGRADE := (9/5)*(FARENHEIT - 32)

END;
```

2.12b   Better

```
FUNCTION CENTIGRADE(FARENHEIT: REAL): REAL;

CONST
   CONVFACTOR = 1.8;
   BASEVALUE  = 32;


BEGIN

   CENTIGRADE := CONVFACTOR*(FARENHEIT - BASEVALUE)

END;
```

Example 2.13 Magic Numbers

2.13a   Poor

```
(*
*   **  FUNCTION TO DETERMINE WHETHER A MAN'S WEIGHT LIES WITHIN
*   **  NORMAL LIMITS, FOR MEN WITH HEIGHTS IN THE RANGE OF
*   **  62 TO 75 INCHES.
*   **
*   **  ON EXIT, WEIGHTCHECK RETURNS:      TOO SHORT
*   **                                     TOO TALL
*   **                                     OVERWEIGHT
*   **                                     UNDERWEIGHT
*   **                                     NORMAL
*)


TYPE
   WEIGHTSTATUS = (TOOSHORT, TOOTALL, OVERWEIGHT, UNDERWEIGHT, NORMAL);

FUNCTION WEIGHTCHECK(HEIGHT, WEIGHT: REAL): WEIGHTSTATUS;

BEGIN

   IF HEIGHT < 62 THEN
      WEIGHTCHECK := TOO SHORT

   ELSE IF HEIGHT > 75 THEN
      WEIGHTCHECK := TOO TALL

   ELSE IF WEIGHT > (133 + 4.3*(HEIGHT - 62)) THEN
      WEIGHTCHECK := OVERWEIGHT

   ELSE IF WEIGHT < (124 + 4*(HEIGHT - 62)) THEN
       WEIGHTCHECK := UNDERWEIGHT

   ELSE
      WEIGHTCHECK := NORMAL

END;
```

2.13b   Better

```
(*
*    **   FUNCTION TO DETERMINE WHETHER A MANS WEIGHT LIES WITHIN
*    **   NORMAL LIMITS, FOR MEN WITH HEIGHTS IN THE RANGE OF
*    **   62 TO 75 INCHES.
*    **
*    **   ON EXIT, WEIGHTCHECK RETURNS:      TOO SHORT
*    **                                      TOO TALL
*    **                                      OVERWEIGHT
*    **                                      UNDERWEIGHT
*    **                                      NORMAL
*)

TYPE
    WEIGHTSTATUS = (TOOSHORT, TOOTALL, OVERWEIGHT, UNDERWEIGHT, NORMAL);


FUNCTION WEIGHTCHECK(HEIGHT, WEIGHT: REAL): WEIGHTSTATUS;

CONST
    MINHEIGHT = 62;
    MAXHEIGHT = 75;
    LOWEIGHT  = 124;
    HIWEIGHT  = 133;
    CONVFAC1  = 4.3;
    CONVFAC2  = 4;


BEGIN

    IF HEIGHT < MINHEIGHT THEN
        WEIGHTCHECK := TOOSHORT

    ELSE IF HEIGHT > MAXHEIGHT THEN
        WEIGHTCHECK := TOOTALL

    ELSE IF WEIGHT > (HIWEIGHT + CONVFAC1*(HEIGHT - MINHEIGHT)) THEN
        WEIGHTCHECK := OVERWEIGHT

    ELSE IF WEIGHT < (LOWEIGHT + CONVFAC2*(HEIGHT - MINHEIGHT)) THEN
        WEIGHTCHECK := UNDERWEIGHT

    ELSE
        WEIGHTCHECK := NORMAL

END;
```

A final issue involved in planning for change concerns the so-called "magic numbers," numbers such as those used in Example 2.13. How many times while reading code have you been stumped by what 75 and 124.0 are all about? A preceding comment line might help, but isn't the alternative of Example 2.13b much better?

The moral is simple: A well-designed program isolates constant data items in a constant declaration. Program modification is made easier, and the reading of the main program is less of a mystery. One will then need a larger and better organized constant declaration, but this is a small, one-time price to pay for the benefits.

Proverb 14   GET THE SYNTAX CORRECT NOW

How many times have you heard the PASCAL language being roundly cursed for its highly sensitive syntax or a PASCAL compiler being criticized for not helping to add "trivial" missing spaces or commas?

Consider the program fragments of Example 2.14a, which contain such trivial syntactic errors. Example 2.14b shows the corresponding corrected versions. (Note: In implementations that relax some of the requirements of standard PASCAL, some of the constructs in Example 2.14a may be legal.) Errors like the ones in the first example should be screened out in advance by a careful programmer. It is our contention that no errors, no matter how trivial, should pass the attention of a good programmer, for it is possible that some of them may not be detected by the compiler and will appear only after a program is in full operation.

Example 2.14 Some Simple Syntactic Errors

2.14a   Wrong

```
(1)   X = X + 1;

(2)   VAR INDEX = INTEGER;

(3)   FOR I = 1, N DO

(4)   X = ((Y*Z) + (C/D) / 4

(5)   PROCEDURE SORT(NAME: ARRAY[1..50] OF REAL);

(6)   PROCEDURE SQUARE(A, Y: REAL);
      BEGIN
          Y := A**2
      END;

(7)   VAR   X, Y, Z: REAL;
          Z := X DIV Y;
```

```
(8)  IF A <> 0
         THEN
             X1 := B + (SQRT((B*B) - (4*A*C)) / (2*A));
             X2 := B - (SQRT((B*B) - (4*A*C)) / (2*A));
         ELSE
             X1 := -C / B;
             X2 := 0;
```

```
(9)  WRITELN ('A POORLY STRUCTURED PROGRAM IS LIKE A SYNTAX, ERROR);
```

2.14b   Correct

```
(1)  X := X + 1;
```

```
(2)  VAR INDEX: INTEGER;
```

```
(3)  FOR I := 1 TO N DO
```

```
(4)  X := ((Y*Z) + (C/D)) / 4;
```

```
(5)  PROCEDURE SORT(NAME: NAMESTRING);
```

```
(6)  PROCEDURE SQUARE(A: REAL; VAR Y: REAL);
     BEGIN
         Y := A*A
     END;
```

```
(7)  VAR X, Y, Z: REAL;
         IF Y <> 0
             THEN
                 Z := X / Y
             ELSE
                 WRITELN('ATTEMPT TO DIVIDE BY ZERO!!!')
```

```
(8)  IF A <> 0
         THEN
             BEGIN
                 X1 := B + (SQRT((B*B) - (4*A*C)) / (2*A));
                 X2 := B - (SQRT((B*B) - (4*A*C)) / (2*A))
             END

         ELSE
             BEGIN
                 X1 := -C/B;
                 X2 := 0
             END;
```

```
(9)  WRITELN('A POORLY STRUCTURED PROGRAM IS LIKE A SYNTAX', ERROR);
```

Furthermore, there is little excuse for syntactic errors in programs, since the manual specifies the syntax for you. The time to consider syntax is not while verifying the completed program but while preparing it. Keep the manual or composite language skeleton handy as you write the code, and if you are not absolutely positive that the syntax of the statement you are writing is perfect, look it up. It only takes a few seconds, and your grasp of the language will increase with constant references to the manual. This work habit is all the more crucial if you are just learning PASCAL or if you have done considerable programming in another language with similar but nevertheless different syntactic constructs.

You can and should write programs that are completely free of syntactic errors on the first run. We mean it. But to do so, you first must convince yourself that indeed you can do it. Second, *you must get someone else to read the work you produce* (see Proverb 19). Just think of all the hours of turn-around time you can waste tracking down simple syntactic errors, not to mention some severe run-time problems that can be caused by "trivial" errors.

Proverb 15 DON'T LEAVE THE READER IN THE DUST

Every programmer has a secret desire to. produce a truly clever program. Shortening the code, running the program faster, or using fewer variables are all popular pastimes. Resist this temptation because the benefits seldom match the hidden costs. A good programmer writes code that is simple to read and quick to the point.

Consider Example 2.15. Each element of code is designed to select the player leading the first card in a card game. Successively higher bids are represented by successively increasing integers. The four-element integer array BID contains the final bids by each of the four players. The players are numbered clockwise from one to four, and the lead player is the person to the left of the highest bidder. Notice that Example 2.15a eliminates several lines of code. Would you use it in your card-playing program?

If you do prefer the program of 2.15a to that of 2.15b, look at both examples carefully. Do you prefer the first because it executes more rapidly or requires less storage? On the computer you regularly use, you may in fact find that Example 2.15b requires less storage, because the loop may take fewer instructions than the straightline code from the corresponding statement in 2.15a. In addition, Example 2.15b may execute faster because no divisions or multiplications are required, and there may be fewer additions. In short, beware of "clever" code, and beware of being penny-wise but pound-foolish.

Example 2.15 Code to Determine Leading Player

2.15a   Tricky Version

```
CONST
   NUMPLAYERS = 4;

VAR
   MAX, LEADER, N: INTEGER;
   BID            : ARRAY[1..NUMPLAYERS] OF INTEGER;


BEGIN

   N :=      (BID[1] DIV MAX)
        + 2*(BID[2] DIV MAX)
        + 3*(BID[3] DIV MAX)
        + 4*(BID[4] DIV MAX);

   LEADER := 1 + (N MOD NUMPLAYERS);

   WRITELN('THE LEADER IS PLAYER NUMBER ', LEADER)


END
```


2.15b   More Natural Version

```
CONST
   NUMPLAYERS = 4;

VAR
   MAX, LEADER: INTEGER;
   BID         : ARRAY[1..NUMPLAYERS] OF INTEGER;


BEGIN

   FOR PLAYER := 1 TO NUMPLAYERS DO
      IF BID[PLAYER] = MAX THEN
         BIDDER := PLAYER;

   IF BIDDER = NUMPLAYERS
      THEN
         LEADER := 1
      ELSE
         LEADER := PLAYER + 1;

   WRITELN('THE LEADER IS PLAYER NUMBER', LEADER)


END
```

To avoid surprises for the reader, a programmer must be conscious that part of his job is to map real world entities (for example prices, temperatures, dollars, dates, and people's names) into the constructs of the PASCAL language (for example, numbers and strings). A programmer must not only choose a particular representation for an entity but must make sure that an operation validly represented in PASCAL has meaning when applied to the original entity. For example, you can perform all arithmetic operations on numeric data. But while you can subtract two dollar amounts to get another dollar amount, it does not make sense to multiply two dollar amounts or to take the square root of a dollar amount.

More generally (see Fig. 2.4), the input to any program represents some class of real world entities: chess squares, wages, row numbers, cards, colors, and the like. A computation is required to transform these entities into other entities; for example, a chess move, an amount of money, a new row number, a card played, another color, and the like. The computer, however, can operate only in limited ways and on a limited set of entities like strings or integers. Thus, it is necessary to transform the real world set of entities and operations into a program containing computer entities and operations. We shall say that a program is "straightforward" or "natural" or "not tricky" if each step in the computer algorithm has a simple correspondence to a step in a real world algorithm that a person would use to solve the problem.

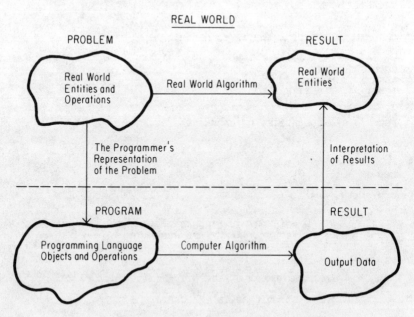

Fig. 2.4   Model for a typical programming task

Straightforwardness and naturalness are closely connected to the clarity and readability of programs. The programmer soon learns that one of the hardest chores of programming is understanding another programmer's code. Often programs do not accurately reflect the real world algorithm corresponding to the numerical, array, logical, or string operations that are required for their computer implementation.

Try looking at any program that you wrote a month ago without peeking at the comments or the documentation. See if you immediately understand all of its details. Now imagine what it would be like for someone else who hadn't seen the program before. Clarity is a godsend to anyone who has to document, debug, extend, use, grade, or otherwise handle a computer program. Unless a program printout is being used by only one person, clarity is a double godsend to anyone having to use the program other than the original programmer.

Example 2.16 Two Card-Counting Algorithms to Find the Rank of a Missing Card

---

2.16a Tricky Card Count

```
CONST
   NUMRANKS = 13;
   NUMCARDS = 51;
   DECKSIZE = 52;

TYPE
   CARDNAME = PACKED ARRAY[1..5] OF CHAR;

VAR
   COUNT: INTEGER;
   RANK : 1..NUMRANKS;
   INDEX: 1..DECKSIZE;

   CARD : CARDNAME;
   DECK : ARRAY[DECKSIZE] OF CARDNAME;

BEGIN


   COUNT := 0;

   FOR INDEX := 1 TO NUMCARDS DO

      BEGIN
         RANK   := GETRANK(DECK[INDEX]);
         COUNT := (COUNT + RANK) MOD NUMRANKS
      END;


   CARD := RANKNAME(NUMRANKS - COUNT);

   WRITELN('THE MISSING CARD IS: ', CARD)


END
```

2.16b   Natural Card Count

```
CONST
   NUMRANKS = 13;
   NUMSUITS = 4;
   NUMCARDS = 51;
   DECKSIZE = 52;

TYPE
   CARDNAME = PACKED ARRAY[1..5] OF CHAR;

VAR
   COUNT: ARRAY[1..NUMRANKS] OF 0..NUMSUITS;
   RANK : 1..NUMRANKS;
   INDEX: 1..DECKSIZE;

   DECK : ARRAY[1..DECKSIZE] OF CARDNAME;
   CARD : CARDNAME;

BEGIN

   FOR RANK := 1 TO NUMRANKS DO
      COUNT[RANK] := 0;

   FOR INDEX := 1 TO NUMCARDS DO
      BEGIN
         RANK := GETRANK(DECK[INDEX]);
         COUNT[RANK] := COUNT[RANK] + 1
      END;

   FOR RANK := 1 TO NUMRANKS DO
      IF COUNT[RANK] < NUMSUITS
         THEN
            CARD := RANKNAME(RANK);

   WRITELN('THE MISSING CARD IS: ', CARD)

END
```

For example, consider the following problem. Given a deck of 51 cards, we are asked to find the rank of the missing card (by computer, of course!). The deck is stored in a 51-element array called DECK. To make things simple, two functions, GETRANK and RANKNAME, are assumed to be defined. GETRANK takes the desired rank of a card as its argument and maps the rank of the card into a number: 1 (for ace), 2 (for deuce), ..., 13 (for king). RANKNAME does the reverse operation. Example 2.16 depicts two pieces of code, both of which claim to do the job correctly. Your problem is to discover *why* each one gives the correct result.

Example 2.16b is obviously correct. In the real world, it corresponds to keeping a checklist of each rank and checking off the card ranks, one by one, until the deck is exhausted. Then the checklist is scanned to find out which card has been checked fewer than four times, and the selected rank is printed.

Example 2.16a is also correct but far less straightforward. It has almost no correspondence to typical card table operations. It runs through the deck keeping a modulo 13 count of all the ranks and afterwards subtracting this count from 13 to get the rank of the missing card. If you are not convinced, try it.

Another area where natural programs have an advantage is that of *extendability*. Because a natural algorithm is analogous to real world operations, extensions using these operations can often be made easily. Since a tricky algorithm usually depends on specific properties of numbers or strings, it usually cannot be applied to cases other than the original problem.

Example 2.17 Extension of the Natural Card Count

```
CONST
    NUMRANKS  = 13;
    NUMSUITS  = 4;
    NUMCARDS  = 51;
    DECKSIZE  = 52;

TYPE
    CARDNAME = PACKED ARRAY[1..5] OF CHAR;

VAR
    COUNT    : ARRAY[1..NUMRANKS] OF 0..NUMSUITS;
    RANK     : 1..NUMRANKS;
    INDEX    : 1..DECKSIZE;

    DECK     : ARRAY[1..DECKSIZE] OF CARDNAME;
    CARD     : CARDNAME;

    NUMISSING: 1..DECKSIZE;

BEGIN

    FOR RANK := 1 TO NUMRANKS DO
        COUNT[RANK] := 0;

    READLN(NUMCARDS);

    FOR INDEX := 1 TO NUMCARDS DO
        BEGIN
            RANK  := GETRANK(DECK[INDEX]);
            COUNT[RANK] := COUNT[RANK] + 1
        END;

    FOR RANK := 1 TO NUMRANKS DO
        IF COUNT[RANK] < NUMSUITS THEN
            BEGIN

                CARD      := RANKNAME(RANK);
                NUMISSING := NUMSUITS - COUNT[RANK];

                WRITELN('THERE ARE ', NUMISSING,
                        CARD, '''S MISSING')

            END

END
```

Example 2.16 illustrates this point well. Say that we now wish to extend the given programs to find the ranks of N missing cards from a deck containing fewer than 51 cards. The algorithm of Example 2.16b can be extended quite readily, as shown in Example 2.17. In the corresponding real world, the sweep of the checklist is the same as before except that when we find that a card is missing, we print it, show that we have covered it by adding it back into the checklist, and see if any others of that rank are missing.

Example 2.16a *cannot* be extended, even to cover the case of two missing cards. The validity of the algorithm is based on the condition that there is only one missing card. With only one missing card, the difference between 13 and the count must be the rank of the missing card. With two or more missing cards, the sum of the ranks of the missing cards may be split in an arbitrary number of ways. In short, this algorithm fails because it is based on the particular properties of numbers instead of the properties of cards.

Before concluding the discussion of this proverb, remember that when tricks are indiscriminately employed, good structure, flexibility, and clarity are frequently lost. Merging two or more modules of code in order to wring out those "extra lines" or adding a few lines in order to gain efficiency are both easy ways to prevent anyone from following the program. Not mentioning the extra time needed to develop the special wrinkle and the extra testing time needed to check the new and often subtle boundary conditions, are you sure that fewer machine instructions or faster machine execution is likely?

One last point about tricky or clever programming must be mentioned. There are cases where tricky methods are in fact justified, for example, to provide demanded efficiency of execution or economy of storage. However, before you resort to tricky programming, you should have a clear reason for doing so. Moreover, you should estimate the actual gain such programming will yield. Otherwise, you should stick to operations and objects that have a natural analog in the real world.

Proverb 16   PRODUCE GOOD OUTPUT

Any experienced programmer engaged in writing programs for use by others knows that, once his program is working correctly, good output is a must. Few people really care how much time and trouble a programmer has spent in designing and debugging a program. Most people see only the results. Often, by the time a programmer has finished tackling a difficult problem, any output may look great. The programmer knows what it means and how to interpret it. However, the same cannot be said for others, or even for the programmer six months hence.

The point is obvious. After all that work and effort spent in writing a program, don't let it look slipshod by having messy, poorly spaced, or skimpy output. Consider Example 2.18a. The output of this simple program could be

Example 2.18 Use of Informative Output

2.18a   Poor

```
CONST
   NUMWEEKS = 4;

TYPE
   SALES = ARRAY[1..NUMWEEKS] OF INTEGER;

VAR
   SALESRECORD            : SALES;
   SALESMAN, AVERAGESALE: INTEGER;
   NUMSALES, INDEX       : 1..NUMWEEKS;


FUNCTION TOTALSALES(SALESRECORD: SALES): INTEGER;

VAR
   INDEX: 1..NUMWEEKS;

BEGIN

   TOTALSALES := 0;

   FOR INDEX := 1 TO NUMWEEKS DO
      TOTALSALES := TOTALSALES + SALESRECORD[INDEX]

END; (* TOTALSALES *)


BEGIN

   READ(SALESMAN);

   FOR INDEX := 1 TO NUMWEEKS DO
      READ(SALESRECORD[INDEX]);
   READLN;

   AVERAGESALE := TOTALSALES(SALESRECORD) / NUMWEEKS;

   WRITELN(SALESMAN, AVERAGESALE);

   FOR INDEX := 1 TO NUMWEEKS DO
      WRITELN(SALESRECORD[INDEX])

END

(*    DATA FOR EXAMPLE 2.18A    *)

   2704  1030   980  1000   990
```

```
(*    OUTPUT FROM EXAMPLE 2.18A    *)

2704  1000
1030
 980
1000
 990
```

2.18b Better

```
CONST
   NUMWEEKS = 4;

TYPE
   SALES = ARRAY[1..NUMWEEKS] OF INTEGER;

VAR
   SALESRECORD          : SALES;
   SALESMAN, AVERAGESALE: INTEGER;
   NUMSALES, INDEX      : 1..NUMWEEKS;

FUNCTION TOTALSALES(SALESRECORD: SALES): INTEGER;

VAR
  INDEX: 1..NUMWEEKS;


BEGIN

   TOTALSALES := 0;

   FOR INDEX := 1 TO NUMWEEKS DO
      TOTALSALES := TOTALSALES + SALESRECORD[INDEX]


END; (* TOTALSALES *)

BEGIN

   READ(SALESMAN);

   FOR INDEX := 1 TO NUMWEEKS DO
      READ(SALESRECORD[INDEX]);
   READLN;

   WRITELN('    SALESMAN ', SALESMAN,' SOLD:');

   FOR INDEX := 1 TO NUMWEEKS DO
      WRITELN('         $', SALESRECORD[INDEX], ' IN WEEK ', INDEX);

   AVERAGESALE := TOTALSALES(SALESRECORD) / NUMWEEKS;

   WRITELN;
   WRITELN('    AVERAGE WEEEKLY SALES  $', AVERAGESALE)

END
```

```
(*   DATA FOR EXAMPLE 2. 18B   *)

   2704   1030   980   1000   990


(*   OUTPUT FROM EXAMPLE 2. 18B   *)

   SALESMAN 2704 SOLD:
      $ 1030 IN WEEK 1
      $  980 IN WEEK 2
      $ 1000 IN WEEK 3
      $  990 IN WEEK 4

   AVERAGE WEEKLY SALES   $ 1000
```

incomprehensible without an exact knowledge of the problem definition or the program itself. The output of the program of Example 2.18b, on the other hand, can be clearly understood by anyone.

The moral is simple. Annotate your output so that its meaning can stand on its own.

Proverb 17   HAND-CHECK THE PROGRAM

It can be difficult to convince a programmer that a program should be hand-checked before being run. Yet run-time errors are the hardest to detect, and unless the system provides excellent debugging facilities, using the computer to help is full of hazards. Even in a time-sharing environment, the programmer is well-advised to check out every program completely by hand before running it. He or she may well be surprised at discovering errors like incorrect signs, infinite loops, and unusual conditions leading to program crashes.

The technique is simple. Choose a sample input, then calculate the output as if you were the computer, assuming nothing and using *exactly* what is written. See that each logical unit performs correctly and that the control sequence through the units is correct. If the program is too long or complex to check in its entirety, then check each major section first, and later check the smaller units, assuming that the major sections are correct. When choosing sample input, take special care to include the boundary conditions and other unusual cases. Failure to account for them is one of the most common programming errors.

For example, suppose you were asked to write a program that takes two nonnegative integers as input—a dividend and a divisor—and prints out two numbers—the integer part of the quotient and the integer remainder.

Assume that PASCAL does not have an integer division operator which gives the integer part of a floating point number. That is, given the integer variables DIVIDEND, DIVISOR, QUOTIENT, and REMAINDER, assume that you cannot just say

QUOTIENT   := DIVIDEND DIV DIVISOR;
REMAINDER := DIVIDEND MOD DIVISOR;

As a first pass, consider the program segment in Example 2.19a. Does this work? Obviously it doesn't, for if it did, it wouldn't be in a proverb called "Hand-Check the Program." Checking by hand, we find that the program bombs out in the WHILE statement. REMAINDER is initially undefined. (Remember, never assume that the computer assumes anything.) We thus change the program as shown in Example 2.19b.

Does the program work now? Obviously not, or we wouldn't have asked. Checking the boundary conditions by hand, we find that when the divisor is zero, the algorithm doesn't terminate. Since division by zero is undefined, we should process this case separately. It wouldn't be wise to leave the program in an infinite loop, computer time costing what it does. We thus change the program as shown in Example 2.19c.

It still doesn't work. Checking another boundary condition, we find that if the divisor exactly divides the dividend, we always get a quotient of 1 less than the correct value. For example, 10 divided by 5 is 2 with a remainder of 0, not 1 with a remainder of 5. Correcting this error is easy, as shown in Example 2.19d.

This version works. Although the first error probably would have been

Example 2.19 Hand-Checking a Program

2.19a   First Attempt

```
VAR
    DIVIDEND, DIVISOR, QUOTIENT, REMAINDER: INTEGER;


BEGIN

    READLN(DIVIDEND, DIVISOR);

    QUOTIENT := 0;

    WHILE (REMAINDER > DIVISOR) DO
        BEGIN
            REMAINDER := REMAINDER - DIVISOR;
            QUOTIENT  := QUOTIENT + 1
        END;

    WRITELN('QUOTIENT = ', QUOTIENT, '    REMAINDER = ', REMAINDER)

END
```

2.19b   Second Attempt

```
VAR
   DIVIDEND, DIVISOR, QUOTIENT, REMAINDER: INTEGER;

BEGIN

   READLN(DIVIDEND, DIVISOR);

   REMAINDER := DIVIDEND;
   QUOTIENT  := 0;

   WHILE (REMAINDER > DIVISOR) DO
      BEGIN
         REMAINDER := REMAINDER - DIVISOR;
         QUOTIENT  := QUOTIENT + 1
      END;

   WRITELN('QUOTIENT = ', QUOTIENT, ' REMAINDER = ', REMAINDER)


END
```

2.19c   Third Attempt

```
VAR
   DIVIDEND, DIVISOR, QUOTIENT, REMAINDER: INTEGER;


BEGIN

   READLN(DIVIDEND, DIVISOR);

   IF DIVISOR = 0
      THEN
         WRITELN('ATTEMPT TO DIVIDE BY 0!!!')

      ELSE
         BEGIN

            REMAINDER := DIVIDEND;
            QUOTIENT  := 0;

            WHILE (REMAINDER > DIVISOR) DO
               BEGIN
                  REMAINDER := REMAINDER - DIVISOR;
                  QUOTIENT  := QUOTIENT + 1
               END;

            WRITELN('QUOTIENT = ', QUOTIENT,    REMAINDER = ', REMAINDER)

         END


END
```

2.19d   Fourth Attempt

```
VAR
    DIVIDEND, DIVISOR, QUOTIENT, REMAINDER: INTEGER;

BEGIN

    READLN(DIVIDEND, DIVISOR);

    IF DIVISOR = 0
        THEN
            WRITELN('ATTEMPT TO DIVIDE BY 0!!!')

        ELSE
            BEGIN

                REMAINDER := DIVIDEND;
                QUOTIENT  := 0;

                WHILE (REMAINDER >= DIVISOR) DO
                    BEGIN
                        REMAINDER := REMAINDER - DIVISOR;
                        QUOTIENT  := QUOTIENT + 1
                    END;

                WRITELN('QUOTIENT = ', QUOTIENT, '  REMAINDER = ', REMAINDER

            END

END
```

picked up easily at run time, the other two probably would not have been. Their effects are input-dependent. Can you imagine searching for a data-dependent error in a long program that goes bad only once in a while?

Simply stated, check your program, especially the boundary conditions, before running it.

Proverb 18   PREPARE TO PROVE THE PUDDING

We have advocated the top-down approach to program development. In turn, we now advocate the top-down approach to checking program correctness, which consists of verifying the main program and the upper levels first and the most primitive modules last.

Verifying from the top down should seem obvious, especially if a program is being written top-down. Programs of this type are usually well modularized, and it is unwise to verify lower levels if the upper levels may be incorrect. Since the sections of the program are integral units that can stand on their own, the most important ones should be verified first. A schematic illustration of a program is presented in Fig. 2.5. Encircled sections indicate that the set of enclosed modules is to be considered as a unit. The program has five main modules, each of which can be verified separately. Some of these modules call submodules, which in turn call other more deeply nested modules. The verification process starts with the main program. As upper modules are verified, the process continues through levels until the entire program has been verified. Verifying the entire program in one lump is to be avoided.

What are some of the available PASCAL verification aids? Foremost, try to write programs that run correctly the first time, and stick to good programming principles. The better the quality of the initial program, the less likely a serious error will occur, and the more likely you will be able to find those errors that do occur.

Second, there is one verification aid in standard PASCAL and on all systems. In computer lingo, it is sometimes known as a "selective dump"; technically, it is known as the WRITE or PRINT statement. These statements can provide snapshots of the program at any point.

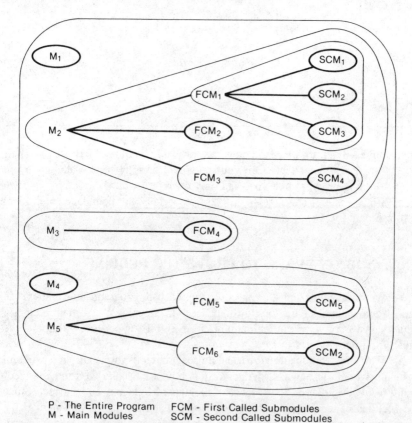

P - The Entire Program   FCM - First Called Submodules
M - Main Modules   SCM - Second Called Submodules

Fig. 2.5 Picture of a program designed top down

Example 2.20 Use of the WRITELN Statement for Verification

```
(*
*   **   PROGRAM TO SUM THE FIRST N POSITIVE INTEGERS
*   **   FOR M INPUT VALUES OF N <= 1000
*)

VAR
    SUM, I, J, M, N: INTEGER;



BEGIN

    SUM := 0;

    READLN(M);

    FOR I := 1 TO M DO

        BEGIN

            READLN(N);

            FOR J := 1 TO N DO
                SUM := SUM + J;

            WRITELN('SUM OF FIRST ', N, '  INTEGERS IS ', SUM)

        END


END


(*   OUTPUT FROM EXAMPLE 2.20   *)

SUM OF FIRST   6   INTEGERS IS      21
SUM OF FIRST   3   INTEGERS IS      27



(*   VERIFICATION LINE INSERTED BEFORE WRITELN STATEMENT:    *)

        WRITELN('ITERATION ', J, '  SUM ', SUM);



(*   OUTPUT FROM EXAMPLE 2.20 WITH VERIFICATION LINE    *)

ITERATION    1    SUM    1
ITERATION    2    SUM    3
ITERATION    3    SUM    6
ITERATION    4    SUM    10
ITERATION    5    SUM    15
ITERATION    6    SUM    21
SUM OF FIRST   6   INTEGERS IS      21
ITERATION    1    SUM    22
ITERATION    2    SUM    24
ITERATION    3    SUM    27
SUM OF FIRST   3   INTEGERS IS      27
```

Consider Example 2.20, a program for summing the first N positive integers for differing values of N. Clearly, the answers generated by the program are incorrect. The programmer decides to check the main program loop and adds the verification lines shown, which print out the inner loop control variable and the current value of the sum. When the revised program is run, we can easily see that on iteration 1 for the second value of N, the sum is already 22; that is, SUM is not properly initialized. Moving the SUM initialization statement to just before the inner FOR loop solves the problem.

One popular verification aid available in several implementations is the "trace." Basically, a trace is a facility which will monitor the behavior of prespecified variables or functions. The trace of a variable can monitor any use or change of its value. The trace of a function can monitor each call, its arguments, and its returned value. The programmer can use a trace to verify that functions are being called with proper arguments and correct returned values. In function-oriented programs or programs with recursion, traces can be invaluable. One word of caution: Overuse of the trace feature has been known to produce voluminous output with no useful information.

Systems that implement PASCAL ordinarily offer other verification facilities. Does your system support any program design, development, or documentation aids? Does your system support a cross-reference lister, program librarian, test data generator, test supervisor, module testing, execution monitor, or output analyzer package? Be sure to find out what features your system provides, and incorporate them into programs you write. Although it may not be wise to use implementation-dependent features as part of a final program, it would be foolish not to utilize them for verification.

In summary, you can and should make good use of the verification facilities in your computer system. Remember, blessed is he who expects the worst, for he shall not be disappointed.

Proverb 19   HAVE SOMEONE ELSE READ THE WORK

This proverb is so important that we considered putting it at the head of the list. Every programmer should realize that programming is by no means a purely personal art. While poor definitions, documentation, and programs can be easy to overlook, they will be quite evident to someone else. Even good programmers stand to gain by having others read the work being produced.

Having someone else read the work does *not* mean just having someone else read the final code. Even a developing problem definition ought to be read by someone else. The program specifications, the levels of the top-down design, and the test plans you are writing should also be read. All of these projects should be doublechecked by someone else.

The primary benefit of this second reading is that it helps weed out quickly all unwarranted assumptions, unintentional omissions, unnecessary complexities, or just plain mistakes. However, there are other benefits. Both you and your reader can learn good problem-solving and programming techniques from one another. Programming teams that make a point of work-reading foster

Example 2.21 The Compiler Catches One Error, But Who Catches the Other?

```
(*
**    **  PROGRAM TO FIND THE REAL ROOTS OF THE EQUATION:
**    **  (A*(X*X)) + (B*X) + C = 0
*)


VAR
    A, B, C, X, X1, X2, DISCRIMINANT: REAL;



BEGIN

    READLN(A, B, C);

    WRITELN('A= ', A, ' B= ', B, ' C= ', C);

    IF A = 0 THEN

       IF B = 0
          THEN
              WRITELN('THIS IS THE DEGENERATE CASE')

          ELSE
            BEGIN
                X := -C / B;
                WRITELN('ONE REAL ROOT... X = ', X)
            END;


    DISCRIMINANT := (B*B) - (4*A*C);

    IF DISCRIMINANT < 0 THEN
       WRITELN('NO REAL ROOTS')

    ELSE IF DISCRIMINANT = 0 THEN
       BEGIN
           X1 := -B/2 * A;
           X2 := X1;
           WRITELN('EQUAL REAL ROOTS:   X1 = ', X1, '  X2 = ', X2)
       END

    ELSE IF DISCRIMINANT > 0 THEN
       BEGIN
           X1 := (-B + SQRT(DISCRIMINANT)) / 2 * A;
           X2 := (-B - SQRT(DISCRIMINANT)) / 2 * A;
           WRITELN('DISTINCT REAL ROOTS:   X1 = ', X1, '  X2 = ', X2)
       END


END
```

cooperative communication, maintain team standards more easily, promote quality documentation, and consistently keep abreast of the total work effort.

Consider Example 2.21, which contains two simple but easily made errors. The programmer who wrote the code would find the errors almost impossible to detect by rereading the code yet another time. Try to find them yourself. We contend that work-reading will help prevent such errors from ever disturbing your sleep.

We have a few suggestions for making work-reading more effective. First, remember the proverbs, and point out any violations you see. Second, choose a sample input; then calculate the output as if you were the computer. Assume nothing and use exactly what is written. See that each module performs correctly. If the program is too long or complex to check in its entirety, then check each major section first, and later check the smaller units, assuming that the major sections are correct. Third, take special care to watch for the boundary conditions and other special cases. Failure to account for these is one of the most critical programming errors.

The time and extra care required for work-reading seem a small price to pay for all the benefits listed above. However, at first the practice may seem time-consuming, annoying, and possibly even embarrassing. You must make an extra effort to stick by this proverb for quite a while. Given time, it will come to have an enormous beneficial impact on your work. As a helpful hint we recommend that you practice as a reader for others. Remember, *all aspects of good programming practice are fostered by work-reading*.

Proverb 20   READ THE MANUALS AGAIN

Now why would anyone want to go back and read those boring language or system manuals again? A wise programmer will occasionally do exactly that. After programming for a while, one tends to restrict oneself to a convenient subset of a language or the host computer system. As a result, many useful features may be neglected. Periodically rereading the manuals will help to keep useful features in mind when the need for them arises.

Do you know how PASCAL deals with character strings? Do you know how integer division works? Do you know all the predefined mathematical functions and the file manipulation capabilities? Does your implementation allow reference to externally compiled procedures? How about the number of significant figures kept by your particular machine? How is the program header defined on your implementation? Can input or output files be structured or segmented? How are the reader and writer functions implemented? What are the default field specifications for output of standard data types? How are carriage control characters defined?

Other features include the use of compiler options, string facilities, and input/output. You must, of course, be careful when using unfamiliar or little-used features. Be sure you are using them correctly. Do not go overboard, for the results may no longer be simple and direct. Nevertheless, we strongly recommend an occasional look at your manuals. You may be pleased with what you find.

Proverb 21 DON'T BE AFRAID TO START OVER

This is the last proverb, but it is of great importance. We dare not dwell on it too long because we hope you will never have to use it.

Sometimes during program development, testing, or modification, it may occur to a programmer that the program he is working with is becoming unusually cumbersome. So many user-requirement changes may have occurred that the problem is now different from what it was originally. Very few, if any, of the programming proverbs may have been applied in developing the program; or perhaps the program produces error after error.

Pruning and restoring a blighted tree is almost an impossible task. The same is true of blighted computer programs. Restoring a structure that has been distorted by patches and deletions or fixing a program with a seriously weak algorithm just isn't worth the time. The best that can result is a long, inefficient, unintelligible program that defies further maintenance. The worst that could result we dare not think of. When you seem hopelessly in trouble, start over. Lessons painfully learned on the old program can be applied to the new one to yield the desired result in far less time with far less trouble.

This last proverb may seem heartless, but don't let your ego stand in the way. Don't be afraid to start over. We mean *really* start over. Don't fall into the trap of trying to convert a bad program into a good one.

EXERCISES

Exercise 2.1   (Define the Problem Completely)
Consider the following program specification:

> "Write a program that computes the weight in kilograms of a weight expressed in pounds and ounces."

Upon careful thought, the above specification reveals many points that would be unclear to a programmer. Rewrite the above specification so that *any* two programs written to solve the problem would have *exactly* the same input–output characteristics, for example, the same input format, the same number of significant digits, the same headings, and so forth. (Note: You are to write a program specification, *not* a program; a good definition may require a full page.)

Exercise 2.2   (Define the Problem Completely)

Each of the following program specifications is either missing one or more critical definitions or is unclear, misleading, or confusing. (a) How are the program specifications deficient? (b) Rewrite all or part of one program specification to make it as clear and explicit as possible, that is, so that there can be no doubt as to what the program should do. (c) In general, what does *any* program specification require to make it as clear and explicit as possible?

Program specification 1: Given the following rates of payment, write a program that will compute the monthly commission for a car salesman.

Grade of Salesman	Commission Rate
1	$5.00 + 0.50% for first ten sales $7.50 + 0.75% every subsequent sale
2	$7.50 + 0.75% for first ten sales $10.00 + 1.00% every subsequent sale
3	$10.00 + 1.00% for first ten sales $12.50 + 1.25% every subsequent sale
4	$12.50 + 1.25% for first ten sales $15.00 + 1.50% every subsequent sale
5	$15.00 + 1.50% for first ten sales $17.50 + 1.75% every subsequent sale

The input should be the grade of the salesman and the number of sales he has made for the month. The output should read "THE SALESMAN'S COMMISSION IS $c," where c is the salesman's commission.

Program specification 2: The Programmer's Equity Life Insurance Company offers policies of $25,000, $50,000, and $100,000. The cost of a policyholder's annual premium is determined as follows. There is a basic fee that depends upon the amount of coverage carried. This is $25 for a $25,000 policy, $50 for a $50,000 policy, and $100 for a $100,000 policy.

In addition to the basic fee, there are two additional charges depending on the age and lifestyle of the policyholder. The first additional charge is determined by multiplying by 2 the policyholder's age minus 21 and then multiplying this by either 1½, 2, or 3 if the policy is at the $25,000, $50,000, or $100,000 level, respectively. The second additional charge is determined by the policyholder's lifestyle, which is a rating of the danger of harm resulting from his occupation and hobbies. This rating is determined by company experts from a questionnaire returned by the policy applicant. They return a rating of from 1 to 5 in steps of 1, with 1 being the safest rating. The charge is then determined by multiplying this rating by 5 and then further multiplying by 1½, 2, or 3 if the policy is either at the $25,000, $50,000, or $100,000 level, respectively. The total premium is found by adding together these separately determined charges.

Write a program to output tables of yearly premium costs for men of ages from 21 to 75 for all amounts of policy value and safety ratings.

Exercise 2.3 (Define the Problem Completely)
Upon careful reading, the problem definition of Example 2.1b shows several deficiencies. The *exact* input–output characteristics are not really fully specified. Describe these deficiencies.

Exercise 2.4 (Use Functions and Subroutines)
Consider a program with the following specification:

> *Input:*   a positive integer N
> *Output:*   the values ΣN, $\Sigma(\Sigma N)$, $\Sigma(\Sigma(\Sigma N))$, and $\Sigma(\Sigma(\Sigma(\Sigma N)))$

where ΣN denotes the sum of the first N integers.

1. Write the program *without* the use of functions or subroutines.
2. Write the program using functions or subroutines. The differences can be quite striking.

Exercise 2.5 (Don't GOTO)
Restructure the following statement sequence to eliminate all GOTOs and statement numbers and to make the sequence as *short* and clear as possible. (Note: It can be done with only two assignment statements.)

```
BEGIN

    GOTO 3;

1:    IF X = 0
        THEN
            GOTO 9
        ELSE
            GOTO 5;

5:    IF X > MAXVALUE
        THEN
            GOTO 6
        ELSE
            GOTO 4;

9:    WRITELN(X);
    GOTO 7;

3:    READLN(X);
    GOTO 1;
```

```
6:    X := SQRT(X);

8:    X := X*X + X;
      GOTO 9;

4:    X := X*X;
      GOTO 8;

7:    . . .

END;
```

Exercise 2.6   (Don't GOTO)

Consider the conventional 8 by 8 array representation of a chessboard whose squares are denoted by (1,1), (1,2), . . . , (8,8) and the problem of placing eight queens on the board so that *no* queen can capture *any other* queen. In chess, a queen can capture another piece if the queen lies on the same row, column, or diagonal as the other piece.

1. Write a program to read in the coordinates of eight queens and print "TRUE" if no queen can capture any other and "FALSE" otherwise.
2. Draw a flow diagram for the program.
3. Score the program according to the following rule:

$$\text{SCORE} = 100 - 10*(\text{number-of-crossing-lines})$$

Exercise 2.7   (Get the Syntax Correct Now)

It is important that a programmer be able to detect simple syntactic errors. Consider the following program to compute PI using the series,

$$PI^4/96 = 1/1^4 + 1/3^4 + 1/5^4 + \ldots.$$

How many syntactic errors are there? Correct the program so that there are no errors.

```
N := 0;

WHILE (ABS(TEMP) EPSILON) DODO
    BEGIN
        N := N + 1
        TEMP := 1 / (2N - 1)**4;
        SUB  := SUM + TEMP
    END;

PI := SQRT(SQRT(DELTA*SUM));
```

Exercise 2.8   (Get the Syntax Correct Now)

Which of the following examples are syntactically correct instances of the given **PASCAL** categories? Correct the erroneous examples. If possible, you should assume *any* suitable specification statements needed to make a construct correct.

(1) ARITHMETIC EXPRESSION

    F(F)

(2) ARITHMETIC EXPRESSION

    P[Q] + X**X**X - 1/2

(3) IF STATEMENT

    IF (X AND Y > 4) WRITELN(X)

(4) FOR STATEMENT

    FOR I = 1 TO N DO
       X[I] := X[I] + X[I]

(5) TYPE DECLARATION

    TYPE BOOLEAN := (TRUE, FALSE);

(6) CASE STATEMENT

    CASE COLOR OF
        RED   := GREEN;
        GREEN := 'GO';
        YELLOW := 'SLOW DOWN';
        RED   := 'STOP'
    END;

(7) FUNCTION

    FUNCTION F(X, Y, Z): REAL;
       F := X * Y + Z
    END;

(8) FUNCTION

    FUNCTION F(X, Y, Z: REAL): REAL;

    VAR SUM: REAL;

    BEGIN

       FOR I := 1 TO Z DO
          SUM := SUM + X[I] + Y[I];

       F := SUM

    END;

Exercise 2.9   (Use Mnemonic Names)

The following statement sequence performs a well-known, simple arithmetic computation. By basically changing all identifiers, rewrite the program so that it clearly illuminates the intended computation.

```
CONST
    FOUR = 4E0;
    FIVE = 5E0;
    AND  = "AND"

VAR
    LEFT, RIGHT, MIDDLE, ALL,
    LEFT1, LFT2, RIGHT1        : REAL;


BEGIN

    WHILE NOT EOF DO
        BEGIN

            READLN(LEFT, MIDDLE, RIGHT);

            RIGHT1 := LEFT*RIGHT*FOUR;
            LEFT1  := MIDDLE*MIDDLE - RIGHT;
            LEFT2  := SQRT(LEFT1);
            ONE    := -(LEFT2 - MIDDLE)/(FIVE*LEFT);
            ALL    := -(LEFT2 - MIDDLE)/(2E0*LEFT);

            WRITELN(ONE, AND, ALL)

        END


    END
```

Exercise 2.10 (Plan for Change)

Consider a program to compute the gravitational force F exerted between two planets M_1 and M_2 located (over time) at different orbital distances from each other. In particular, let

$$M_1 = \text{mass of planet } 1 = 6 \times 10^{24}$$
$$M_2 = \text{mass of planet } 2 = 8 \times 10^{25}$$
$$G = \text{gravitational constant} = 6.7 \times 10^{-11}$$
$$F = G * M_1 * M_2 / (R \uparrow 2)$$

Write a program to output F for values of R varying from $100 * 10^8$ to $110 * 10^8$ in increments of $0.01 * 10^8$ such that all constants are specified in a data statement and *no* constant terms are recomputed.

Exercise 2.11 (Produce Good Output)

The following input/output was generated by the use of a working program in a time-sharing environment:

> *Input:* WHAT IS N1 AND N2?
> 5, 10

Output:	5	25
	6	36
	7	49
	8	64
	9	81
	10	100

Rewrite the input/output so that the average ''man on the street'' would be able to understand what the input numbers 5 and 10 represent and what the output means.

Exercise 2.12   (Have Someone Else Read the Work)
Describe two more advantages to having someone else read the work you produce during the various phases of a programming project (see Proverb 19). Describe two disadvantages or bottlenecks.

Exercise 2.13   (Read the Manuals Again)
Reread your PASCAL manual and find three features that you had forgotten or did not know existed. For each feature give an example of how it would be most useful.

Exercise 2.14   (Read the Manuals Again)
Answer precisely the following questions with reference to your PASCAL manual:

1. What are the spacing conventions that enable or prohibit prettyprinting?
2. How many dimensions can an array have?
3. What is a legal subscript?
4. In what contexts can the logical values of TRUE and FALSE appear?
5. Are matrix commands available?
6. How many significant digits are kept for REAL numbers?

Exercise 2.15   (Several Proverbs)
The following program performs a simple, well-known computation. Rewrite the program so that it clearly illuminates the intended computation. In the process, eliminate GOTOs, use mnemonic names, and produce good output.

```
VAR
    A, B, C, D, F, G : REAL;

BEGIN

    GOTO 1;
```

```
2:  READLN(A);
    F := A * A;
    GOTO 3;

1:  READLN(B);
    G := B * B;
    GOTO 2;

3:  IF (A <= 0) OR (B <= 0)
        THEN
            GOTO 5

    ELSE
        BEGIN
            C := F + G;
            D := SQRT(C);
            WRITELN(D)
        END

5:  ...

END
```

Exercise 2.16   (Several Proverbs)

Write a program that determines whether an input string is a palindrome. A palindrome is a string that reads the same forwards and backwards. For example, LEVEL is a palindrome but PALINDROME is not. When the program is running correctly, score it using the following formula:

$$\text{SCORE} = 100 - (5*\text{times-resubmitted})$$
$$- (2*\text{number-of-lines-changed})$$

Exercise 2.17   (Several Proverbs)

Usually, a complex mathematical expression can be coded as a single arithmetic expression. However, for the sake of clarity it is often advantageous to split up a lengthy arithmetic expression and use intermediate variables. Give an example where clarity is gained with the use of intermediate variables. Give an example where the obvious result is program efficiency. Give an example where the use of inappropriate or excessive intermediate variables causes confusion.

Exercise 2.18   (Guess the Proverb)

The following program is supposed to have the following characteristics:

Input: a sequence of non-zero integers terminated by the integer zero
Output: the MEAN

$$(\sum_{i=1}^{n} x_i) / n$$

and standard deviation,

$$\text{SQRT}(\; (\sum_{i=1}^{n} x^2) \, / \, n \; - \; \text{MEAN}^2)$$

of the integers in the input sequence.

```
VAR
    A, B, C   : INTEGER;
    D, E, F, G: REAL;


BEGIN

    A := 0;  B := 0;  C := 0;  D := 0;
    D := 0;  E := 0;  F := 0;

    REPEAT

        WHILE NOT EOF DO
            BEGIN
                READLN(G);

                A := A + G;
                B := B + 1;
                C := C + SQR(G)
            END

        UNTIL G <= F;


    D := A/B;
    E := SQRT(C/B - SQR(A));
    I := F - D/F;

    WRITELN(E, E)


END
```

Of all the programming proverbs, which *single* proverb, if properly followed, would be most valuable in converting the above program to a good
program? (Note: There really *is* a best answer.)

Exercise 2.19 (The PASCAL quiz)

A user who has a *very thorough* knowledge of any language should be able
to detect erroneus programs that prematurely terminate because of a syntactic (compile-time) or semantic (run-time) error. In the absence of a formal
definition of a language, the definition of constructs that produce fatal
syntactic or semantic errors must ultimately be based on a particular implementation. To treat this issue precisely, consider the insertion of print
statements as the first and last executable statements in a program, and let
us adopt the following definitions:

1. A program is "syntactically invalid" if the first print statement is not executed, that is, if the compiler finds an unacceptable error.
2. A program is "syntactically valid" if the first print statement is executed, that is, if the compiler detects no severe errors, translates the program into machine language, and begins execution.
3. A program is "semantically invalid" (but syntactically valid) if the first but not the last print statement is executed, that is, if the program is compiled and execution is started but not completed.
4. A program is "semantically valid" (and syntactically valid) if the first and last print statements are executed, that is, if the program is compiled and executed without abnormal termination.

To test your knowledge of the above issues in PASCAL, you are asked to answer two simple questions about the programs given in the PASCAL quiz below.

Is the first WRITE statement (which prints "START") executed?
Is the last WRITE statement (which prints "FINISH") executed?

Check the appropriate spaces or put your answers on a separate sheet. (Note: It is quite difficult to answer all questions correctly.)

```
(1)   START  -  YES__  NO__     (2)   START  -  YES__  NO__
      FINISH -  YES__  NO__           FINISH -  YES__  NO__

      VAR   A, B, C: INTEGER;         VAR  X: REAL;

      BEGIN
                                      FUNCTION P(FUNCTION F: REAL): REAL;
          WRITELN('START');
                                      BEGIN
          A := 1;                       P := F(1.4, 2.6, 1.8)
      6:  B := 2;                     END;

          GOTO 6;
                                      BEGIN
      6:  C := 33;
                                          WRITELN('START');
          WRITELN('FINISH')
                                          X := P(MAX);
      END
                                          WRITELN('FINISH')

                                      END
```

```
(3)  START  - YES__ NO__          (4)  START  - YES__ NO__
     FINISH - YES__ NO__               FINISH - YES__ NO__


     VAR A: REAL;                      VAR  A: REAL;

     PROCEDURE P(VAR X, Y: REAL);      PROCEDURE P(VAR X, Y: REAL);

     BEGIN                             BEGIN
        X := X + 1;                       X := X + 1;
        Y := Y*(X + 1)                    Y := Y*(X + 1)
     END;                              END;

     BEGIN                             BEGIN

        WRITELN('START');                 WRITELN('START');

        A := 2;                           A := 2;
        P(A, 1);                          P (A, TRUE);

        WRITELN('FINISH')                 WRITELN('FINISH')

     END                               END
```

```
(5)  START  - YES__NO__
     FINISH - YES__NO__


     VAR  J: INTEGER;


     FUNCTION G(FUNCTION F: INTEGER;  N: INTEGER): INTEGER;

     VAR   F, N: INTEGER;

     BEGIN
        IF N = 0
           THEN
              G := 1
           ELSE
              G := N*F (F, N-1)
     END;

     FUNCTIONFACT(N: INTEGER): INTEGER;

     BEGIN
        FACT := G(G, N)
     END;

     BEGIN

        WRITELN('START');

        J := FACT(5);

        WRITELN('FINISH')

     END
```

CHAPTER THREE
TOP-DOWN PROGRAMMING

"There is a certain method in this madness."

Horace: *Satires* II.iii

This chapter presents a technique of program development generally known as top-down programming. The top-down approach presented here is based on the notions of "structured programming" of Dijkstra [Ref. D1] and "stepwise refinement" [Ref. W2]. While the technique is not a panacea for all programming ills, it does offer strong guidelines for an intelligent approach to a programming problem.

Before coding, every programmer must have in hand a complete statement of the problem, a well-planned documentation system, and a clear design strategy. The input format, legal and illegal fields, output files, reports, program messages, and the mapping from all various input data situations to their correct outputs must be described in detail. Furthermore, the overall algorithm must also be determined before coding. It is senseless to start coding a program without such a complete attack on the problem.

Given a solid problem definition and an overall program design, the top-down approach is a method for developing computer programs in any programming language. In brief, the approach has the following characteristics:

1. *Design in Levels*. The programmer designs the program in *levels,* where a level consists of one or more modules. A module is always "complete," although it may reference unwritten submodules. The first level is a complete "main program." A lower level refines or develops unwritten modules in the upper level. In other words, the modules of a successive level consist of the submodules referenced in the prior level. The programmer may look several levels ahead to determine the best way to design the level at hand.

2. *Initial Language Independence*. The programmer initially uses expressions (often in English) that are relevant to the problem solution, even though the expressions cannot be directly transliterated into code. From statements that are machine and language independent, the programmer moves toward a final machine implementation in a programming language.

3. *Postponment of Details to Lower Levels*. The programmer concentrates on critical broad issues at the initial levels and postpones details (for example, choice of specific algorithms or intermediate data representations) until lower levels.

4. *Formalization of Each Level*. Before proceeding to a lower level, the programmer ensures that the "program" in its current stage of development is a "formal" statement. In most cases, this means a program that calls unwritten submodules with all arguments spelled out. This step ensures that further sections of the program will be developed independently, without having to change the specifications or the interfaces between modules.

5. *Verification of Each Level*. After generating the modules of a new level, the programmer verifies the developing formal statement of the program. This ensures that errors pertinent to the current level of development will be detected at their own level.

6. *Successive Refinements*. Each level of the program is refined, formalized, and verified successively until the programmer obtains a completed program that can be transformed easily into code.

One should note several things about the top-down approach. First, the entire problem and its overall solution are presumed to be understood (see Proverbs 1 through 4). It is senseless to start programming until there is a complete understanding of the problem and a complete general plan of attack. Such an understanding allows the programmer to write the program without losing sight of the overall goal.

Second, at the upper levels, the approach is machine and language independent, and the programmer is not constrained by the details of a programming language. He or she is writing the upper levels using a notation that meaningfully solves the problem, although it might not be understood by a language processor. The programmer's use of a particular notation involves no sacrifice. At each level the statements produced still represent a complete program in some sense. All that is lacking is the machine capable of executing the statements.

Third, at each level of design, informal notation must be formalized as a hypothetical, but explicitly specified, procedure. Specification involves a complete listing of all input and output arguments.

Fourth, at each level the programmer must verify the program in its present form so that further refinements will be absolutely correct with respect to previously designed levels. This ensures that oversights will be detected in their proper context.

For example, suppose that a programmer is working at an intermediate level and generates the following informal statement:

case day-of-the-week *of*

Monday:	generate last week's data summary
Tuesday:	do nothing
Wednesday:	update usage file
Thursday:	process new data
Friday:	generate lab item reports
Saturday:	generate weekly breakage statistics
Sunday:	do nothing

end

The language of this statement is far removed from a programming language. On the other hand, the statement is perfectly clear to the programmer in that it reflects a portion of the desired code. The programmer must elaborate on the required inputs and expected outputs for the procedures like "generate lab item reports" and "update usage file." The next levels of refinement must develop each procedure.

The process of solving a problem using the top-down approach can be graphically represented by two trees. The first of them, illustrated in Fig. 3.1, represents the overall program development process. The top-most level, P_0, represents the general conception of the problem. The branches at each successive level of the tree represent the alternative design decisions that the programmer can make. The paths down the tree represent all possible correct programs to solve the given problem. The top-down approach allows the programmer to make design decisions starting from the P_0 level and to follow the tree downward with successive refinements to construct a good solution. At each level the programmer examines the alternative branches and chooses the one that

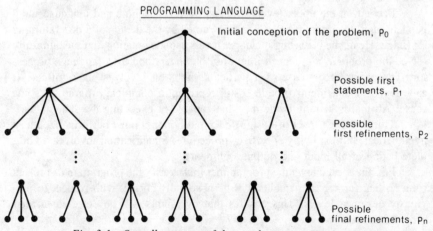

PROGRAMMING LANGUAGE

Initial conception of the problem, P_0

Possible first statements, P_1

Possible first refinements, P_2

Possible final refinements, P_n

Fig. 3.1   Overall structure of the top-down programming process

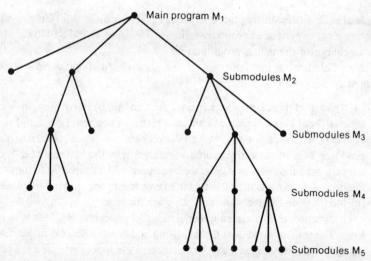

Fig. 3.2   Top-down structure for a specific program

appears most suitable. However, if at any time the choice of any branch seems unwise, it is possible to backtrack up the tree one or more levels and select an alternative solution. The top-down process for a specific problem is thus a sequence of design decisions from P_0 to a specific final program.

The second tree illustrating the top-down approach, shown in Fig. 3.2, represents the hierarchical structure of a specific program for which five levels were needed. The top node is the main program, and the nodes at each successive level are the refined submodules that were introduced but undeveloped in the prior level. By the time the bottom level is reached, we have all the modules that comprise the final program.

There is, of course, a correspondence between the two trees. A single path from P_0 to a particular design choice in P_n in Fig. 3.1 is expanded and described in detail in Fig. 3.2.

The top-down approach is a programming technique that can be widely applied for good results. The technique does not necessarily guarantee the best solution, but it does provide a good structure for solving programming problems. The rest of this chapter will be devoted to an example that illustrates precisely how the top-down method is used to write well-structured modular programs. The example also demonstrates that the method is, by and large, language independent.

KRIEGSPIEL CHECKERS

General Nicklaus C. Roht, President of the state of Atad, has just purchased a Universal 6 computer for his small country. He decides that the first programming job must be performed for the state's national game, Kriegspiel checkers. The General's chairperson of the commission on recreational activities, Charles D. Coleman, is placed in charge of the project. Mr. Coleman puts the state's most experienced program designer, Dr. Irene B. "Top-Down" Malcolm, in charge of the actual programming.

Mr. Coleman, a loyal servant of the state of Atad, prepares a general statement of the problem.

> In Kriegspiel checkers* each player sits in an isolated area, having a separate board containing only his own pieces. Each move must follow the conventional rules for the game of checkers. However, as each player proposes a move, a third person, the referee, tells the player that either (a) the proposed move is legal, and the opponent will be directed to move; (b) the proposed move is illegal, and the player must propose another move; or (c) the proposed move wins and the game is over.
>
> Using the conventional rules for Kriegspiel checkers, each game is quite long. The state of Atad uses the following additional rules: (a) In addition to winning a game by capturing or blocking all of the opponent'e pieces, a player also wins by getting the first king. (b) When a player proposes a legal jump that is part of a multiple jump, the referee informs the player that a further jump is required and the next square must be entered; the player then continues to propose further squares until the multiple jump is completed.
>
> The program must "know" and enforce the rules of checkers, that is, ensure that black always moves first, insist that a jump be made when one is possible, verify the legality of moves, determine when the game is over, and so forth.
>
> Furthermore, the program must accept moves in a format familiar to the players. A move consists of two numbers corresponding to squares on a standard checkerboard. The first number denotes the square of the moving piece, and the second number is its destination square. The program must also output "messages" based on whether the proposed move is legal or not, requires a jump continuation, or terminates the game.
>
> On top of all this, the General insists that the program be operational five weeks from Friday.

As an aid, a picture of a numbered checkerboard has been supplied by Mr. Coleman. This is given in Fig. 3.3.

FUNCTIONAL SPECIFICATION

A professional programmer and a strong advocate of the top-down approach, Irene is calm in the face of General Roht's demands. Despite the fact that a program must be ready in five weeks, she has seen too many programming delays and poor programs caused by a poor problem analysis. Since she is facing

---

*For readers who play checkers, the Kriegspiel variant is much more interesting than it at first appears.

BLACK

RED

Fig. 3.3   Standard checkerboard numbering system

a tight schedule, Irene feels all the more strongly that she must revise the given definition and get as complete a functional specification as possible.

Irene realizes that the inputs for the Kriegspiel program are quite simple. Nevertheless she knows that it is all too easy to overlook some critical cases and she therefore decides to examine them in some detail. In simple form, the inputs are a series of pairs of numbers: The first number represents the square designating a player's piece, and the second number represents the square to which that piece is to be moved. Of course, some of the pairs representing a move will result in a move that is illegal on a given board configuration.

Irene quickly notices that the players might input numbers that are too large to correspond with a square on the checkerboard. She decides to keep a list of such possibilities on her "undesired events list." Further, she is aware that users can easily make typographical errors. As such, it is possible that some of the proposed moves may contain characters that are not numbers at all. She adds this possibility to her list.

With these two simple cases in mind, Irene knows that she must think quite carefully about the kinds of errors the users can make in using this program. The human engineering of this program is very important to Irene. What if the user inputs no separator between square numbers? What if the user inputs too many numbers? What if the user accidently hits a carriage return and inputs no square number at all? After some thought, Irene decides to spell out carefully all of the possible input situations. She itemizes these in the form of a table, which is given in Figure 3.4. Of some note, she decides to allow any trailing string of characters to be given after a proposed move; this allows a player to annotate a game with running comments.

Irene now feels comfortable enough to specify the required outputs for the program. For this program, the outputs are indeed simple, merely messages printed to each player. There are many possible messages, and she believes that it is important to determine these messages now. After all, they really should be

Input Field	Possible Values	Error Conditions
Normal (2-square) move		
Leading string	Empty	None
First square number	$1 \leq$ integer ≤ 32	Number too large or too small; contains a non-numeric character
Separator string	A space or comma	Does not contain a space or comma
Second square number	$1 \leq$ integer ≤ 32	Number too large or too small; contains a non-numeric character
Trailing string	Any string of characters	None
Jump Continuation (1-square) Move		
Leading string	Empty	None
First square number	$1 \leq$ integer ≤ 32	Number too large or too small; contains a non-numeric character
Trailing string	Any string of characters	None

Fig. 3.4   Format for input lines to Kriegspiel program

approved by Mr. Coleman. There are messages indicating that a move must be entered by a player, that a move is legal, that a move is illegal, that a move contains characters that are not understandable by the program, that a square number is out of range, that a move is a jump and requires further inputs, and that the game is won by one of the players.

Irene decides that most messages should be short, for after repetitive use, frequent long messages can be quite annoying to a player. Furthermore, some of the messages should give the user quite specific information, especially in those cases where the user makes an error. She prepares a complete list of output messages for the program, and itemizes these messages in the form of a table, given in Figure 3.5.

Having completed the details of the format and contents of the various inputs and outputs, Irene now describes the mapping of input situations into output responses. Such a description is invaluable to the programmer who develops the ultimate program. Irene's description, given in Figure 3.6, consists of nested conditions that describe the actions and output response to each input.

The functional specification of user requirements is done! Irene happily reviews her results and collects them into a draft for the documentation manual. A copy is sent to Mr. Coleman. Irene drops off other copies to members of the

Reason for Message	Message
Introductory message for player with black pieces	WELCOME TO KRIEGSPIEL CHECKERS ENTER YOUR FIRST MOVE XX XX
Introductory message for player with red pieces	WELCOME TO KRIEGSPIEL CHECKERS YOUR OPPONENT WILL TAKE THE FIRST MOVE
Prompt player for a normal (2-square) move	IT'S YOUR TURN TO MOVE XX XX
Prompt player for a (1-square) jump continuation	YOUR JUMP MUST BE CONTINUED ENTER JUMP SQUARE XX
Acknowledge legal move	YOU HAVE COMPLETED A LEGAL MOVE AND YOUR OPPONENT HAS BEEN ASKED TO MOVE
Nonnumeric characters in input square	NONNUMERIC CHARACTERS IN SQUARE
Illegal square number	SQUARE NUMBER OUT OF RANGE
No space or comma between square numbers	NO SPACE OR COMMA BETWEEN SQUARES
Jump exists and has not been taken	A JUMP IS AVAILABLE AND YOU MUST TAKE IT
Illegal move	TRY AGAIN XX XX
Illegal jump continuation	ILLEGAL JUMP CONTINUATION
Piece captured	PIECE CAPTURED FROM SQUARE
Losing message	SORRY . . . YOUR OPPONENT HAS WON THE GAME!!!
Winning message	CONGRATULATIONS . . . YOU HAVE WON THE GAME!!!

Fig. 3.5   Output messages for Kriegspiel program

operations board and to one or two of her colleagues for a quick but careful review. Top-down development cannot begin until all criticisms and problems are disposed of.

Just as she is finishing the condition-action table, a new programmer, Dorothy E. Clark, drops in and notices the amount of work Irene is faced with. "Why are you bothering with all this?" she asks. "In college, I was told to try to keep things as short and simple as possible." Irene replies that any evident complexity was not introduced by her but exists in the problem itself. The definition of the problem will not be perfect—what is?—but it will be so close

Action   Print introductory message to each player, and prompt
             player for a normal (2-square) move.

Condition 1   Game has not been won and a normal (2-square) move is
                  required.
  Action   Prompt player for a normal (2-square) move.

  Condition 1.1   First field of input line is not a number.
    Action   Print message indicating illegal characters.
  Condition 1.2   First field is a number that is not a legal square number.
    Action   Print message indicating square number out of range.
  Condition 1.3   Separator is not a blank or comma.
    Action   Print message indicating illegal separator.
  Condition 1.4   Second field is not a number.
    Action   Print message indicating illegal characters.
  Condition 1.5   Second field is not a legal square number.
    Action   Print message indicating illegal square number.
  Condition 1.6   Second field is a legal square number.
  Condition 1.6.1   Move is illegal on the current board configuration.
    Action   Print message indicating illegal move.
  Condition 1.6.2   Move is a legal nonjump but a jump exists.
    Action   Print message that a jump must be taken.
  Condition 1.6.3   Move is a legal nonjump.
    Action   Print message indicating a completed legal move, process
                      the move, and prompt the opponent.
  Condition 1.6.4   Move is a legal jump and does not require a continuation.
    Action   Print message indicating that a piece was captured and
                      that a legal move has been completed, process the move,
                      and prompt the opponent.
  Condition 1.6.5   Move is a legal jump and requires a continuation.
    Action   Print message indicating that a piece was captured, and
                      process a jump continuation.

Condition 2   Game has not been won and a jump continuation (1-
                  square) move is required.
  Action   Prompt player for a jump continuation (1-square) move.

  Condition 2.1   The jump square field is not a number.
    Action   Print message indicating illegal characters.
  Condition 2.2   The jump square field is not a legal square number.
    Action   Print message indicating square out of range.
  Condition 2.3   The jump continuation square is not legal.
    Action   Print message for illegal jump continuation.

Condition 2.4 The jump continuation square is legal.
  Action Print message acknowledging legal continuation and process move.

Condition 3 Game has been won.
  Action Print winning and losing messages.

Fig. 3.6 Mapping of input situations to output responses for Kriegspiel checkers program

---

that it is unlikely that programming changes will have to be made later during top-down development or coding. Irene also points out that thinking now will not only save time later but, more important, will help produce a better program. In addition, a careful functional specification will describe the system as seen by the user. Both Mr. Coleman and the operations board have a *complete* description of the external characteristics of the entire program.

Irene is exhausted after writing the functional specification. Since it is almost 4 o'clock anyway, she decides to leave early for a weekend conference dealing with advances in programming languages.

TOP-DOWN PROGRAM DEVELOPMENT

When Irene returns on Monday, she decides to bring in Dorothy Clark to do the actual top-down development of the Kriegspiel program. Irene meets with Dorothy and explains that the problem is fully specified. Moreover, as a part of normal practice, she tells Dorothy that they will work together closely at the beginning of the top-down development. Irene gives Dorothy a copy of the draft functional specifications and a brief exposition of the top-down approach to programming. She asks Dorothy to give these a careful reading and return the day after next to begin the actual work.

When Dorothy returns, she surprises Irene with the following initial top-down development of the program, P_1:

P_1 *(First pass)*

initialize program variables

10   get a proposed move

if move is legal
  then process the move
  else goto 10

if the game is not over
  then change players and *goto* 10

end the game and stop

Irene is pleased but notes some problems with the first pass. First, Dorothy's P_1 mentions the initialization of some program variables but does not specify which variables are to be initialized and which messages are to be printed. Second, no mention is made of whether a legal move is in fact a part of a jump situation in which the player must input the squares to continue the jump. In addition, "process the move" is a nebulous subroutine, one that even Dorothy will admit is in need of formalization. Third, Irene is disturbed by the GOTO and points out that the real idea is to think about programming without GOTOs in the first place. Irene and Dorothy therefore work together to produce the following revision:

$$P_1 \ (Formal)$$

INITIALIZE (PLAYER,BOARD)
write (INTRODUCTORY__MESSAGES)

repeat

  get (MOVE) from PLAYER

  if LEGAL__MOVE (PLAYER,BOARD,MOVE) *then*
      UPDATE__BOARD (PLAYER,BOARD,MOVE)

      if LEGAL__JUMP (PLAYER,BOARD,MOVE) *and*
      JUMP__CAN__BE__CONTINUED (PLAYER,BOARD,MOVE)
      then
          CONTINUE__THE__JUMP (PLAYER,BOARD,MOVE)

      if NO__KING (BOARD,PLAYER) *and*
      MOVES__LEFT (BOARD,OPPONENT)
      then
          swap PLAYERS
          prompt OPPONENT for next MOVE
     else
          write (WINNING__MSG) for PLAYER
          write (LOSING__MSG) for OPPONENT
          GAME__OVER is TRUE

  else
      write (ILLEGAL__MOVE__MSG) for PLAYER

until GAME__OVER

Irene is still not pleased with this version of the program. For one thing, the current version calls for one subroutine to check for a legal move and a later subroutine to check if the legal move was a jump and the jump can be continued. At a high level concern for efficiency, it is clear to Irene that the check for a legal move must also include a check for a jump which may need to be continued if it is part of a multiple jump. So why recompute this frequently executed test after the move has already been determined to be legal? She decides that the best course of action is to have a single subroutine to check for the legality of the move and return two flags, one that indicates whether the move was legal and one that indicates whether the jump must be continued.

Irene notes another major concern affecting the clarity and efficiency of the entire program. Passing BOARD as a parameter to almost every function and subroutine is somewhat inefficient. Furthermore, the general use of the BOARD variable is obvious. She decides that BOARD should not be passed as an explicit argument to each function and subroutine. Hence, BOARD will be made global and dropped from the argument lists.

Irene also notices a slight error in the current version of P_1. The variable OPPONENT occurs in the code but has never been given a value. Obviously, the OPPONENT is the other PLAYER. In addition, GAME__OVER has not been initialized. These points must be spelled out.

Irene deliberately postpones decisions about data representations for the board and the players. Such decisions are usually limiting, since there is a tendency to program around the properties of the representation.

With these and other considerations Dorothy and Irene agree on the final version P_1. Cautioned by the unobserved bug in P_1, they carefully check the final version of P_1 to ensure that the "program" at this level is indeed correct.

P_1 *(Final pass)*

```
global variable BOARD

INITIALIZE (BOARD)
PLAYER     := BLACK
OPPONENT  := RED

write (INTRODUCTORY__MESSAGES)
GAME__OVER := FALSE
```

repeat

```
    get (MOVE) from PLAYER

    EVALUATE__MOVE
```

using (PLAYER,MOVE)
giving (LEGAL__MOVE__FLAG, MORE__JUMPS__FLAG)

if (LEGAL__MOVE__FLAG is on) *then*
UPDATE__BOARD (PLAYER,MOVE)

if (MORE__JUMPS__FLAG is on) *then*
CONTINUE__THE__JUMP (PLAYER,MOVE)

if NO__KING (PLAYER) and MOVES__LEFT (OPPONENT)
then
write (LEGAL__MOVE__MSG) for PLAYER
write (MAKE__MOVE__MSG) for OPPONENT
swap (PLAYER,OPPONENT)
else
write (WINNING__MSG) for PLAYER
write (LOSING__MSG) for OPPONENT
GAME__OVER := TRUE

else

write (ILLEGAL__MOVE__MSG) for PLAYER

until GAME__OVER

Data Representation

Before Dorothy and Irene can proceed, they must determine the "specific structure of the data representations." This six-dollar phrase means that they must figure out a way to represent the checkerboard and the players' pieces in the program. Remember that players use the standard checkerboard of Fig. 3.3. There is a great temptation to code the standard checkerboard numbering system directly into the program, but Irene points out that this is much more difficult than it appears.

First, look at square 10 of Fig. 3.3. A black piece on that square can make a nonjump move to squares 14 or 15. So the possible moves are $(10 + 4) = 14$, and $(10 + 5) = 15$, or simply $+4$ and $+5$. But from square 15 the black moves are to squares 18 and 19, or simply $+3$ and $+4$. A similar situation exists for red, except that the moves are $-3,-4$ and $-4,-5$, since the move direction is reversed. They could sort out which moves use the 3,4 rule and which moves use the 4,5 rule, but another problem remains. Black's first row (squares 1 through 4) uses the $+4,+5$ rule. But what about square 4? Using the $+4,+5$ rule, 8 is a legal square, but 9 is not.

Dorothy remembers an article she read in *Scientific American* [Ref. S2] that described an ingenious representation for a checkerboard devised by A. L. Samuels (see Fig. 3.7). In this scheme, regardless of the square, the possible directed moves for black are always +4 and +5, and for red, −4 and −5. The added border squares are "flag" squares. They will contain some value to indicate that they do not represent legal squares. When a proposed move goes from a legal square to a "flag" square, the move can be quickly detected as illegal. The opposite border squares are labeled with the same numbers. This causes no confusion as they are flag squares and need not have distinct numbers.

Although this representation solves many problems, Irene is somewhat troubled. Players use the standard checkerboard in Fig. 3.3, whereas the program must use that of Fig. 3.7. This inconsistency means that input moves will have to be converted to Samuel's representative. Furthermore, the whole situation is somewhat tricky to handle. Irene recalls the proverb, "Think First, Code Later," and decides to give the matter a few days "incubation" time.

Thinking and Problem Solving

Dorothy does some hard thinking.

After some time, she realizes that the board has two distinct uses: as a record of the current status of the game, and as a means for determining legal squares for proposed moves. She notes that, aside from player or opponent pieces on the actual board, the possible legal squares for a player's moves are constant. Constant! Yes! Why not let the possible legal square from each square be stored

Fig. 3.7 Samuel's board numbering for internal representation of a checkerboard

Square	Left adjacent square	Right adjacent square	Left jump square	Right jump square
BLACK				
1	5	6	—	10
2	6	7	9	11
3	7	8	10	12
4	8	—	11	—
5	—	9	—	14
.	.	.	.	.
.	.	.	.	.
.	.	.	.	.
31	—	—	—	—
32	—	—	—	—
RED				
1	—	—	—	—
2	—	—	—	—
.	.	.	.	.
.	.	.	.	.
.	.	.	.	.
28	24	—	19	—
29	—	25	—	22
30	25	26	21	23
31	26	27	22	24
32	27	28	23	—

Fig. 3.8   Table of legal adjacent squares for each player. Dashes represent illegal moves

in a constant array? For example, for a black piece on square 14, the only possible nonjumps are to squares 17 and 18, and the only possible jumps are to squares 21 and 23. As for the current status of the game, she can maintain a separate array to keep track of the current board configuration.

She quickly sketches out this idea in the form of a table, which is given in Fig. 3.8. She notes that some left or right moves have no legal square. This causes no problems, for she can easily have a special value for this case. As for the status of the board, she can represent the conventional (32-square) board layout in the form of a 32-element array.

Irene also notes that the status of a proposed move (legal, illegal, jump, nonjump, jump that requires a continuation, etc.) can be nicely represented in PASCAL as a variable whose type is a *set* of scalars where the values represent these conditions.

With these design decisions behind them, Dorothy and Irene can now write P_2, the complete main "program":

P₂ (Refinement of P₁)

global variable BOARD

global "constants" LEGAL＿BLACK＿MOVES＿MAPPING
                   LEGAL＿RED＿MOVES＿MAPPING

 initialize globals

PLAYER   := BLACK
OPPONENT   := RED

write (INTRODUCTORY＿MESSAGES)

GAME＿OVER := FALSE

repeat

   get (OLD＿SQ, NEW＿SQ) from PLAYER

   EVALUATE＿MOVE
     using (PLAYER,OLD＿SQ,NEW＿SQ)
     giving (MOVE＿STATUS)

   if (LEGAL ＿ MOVE in MOVE ＿ STATUS) *then*
      UPDATE＿BOARD (PLAYER,OLD＿SQ,NEW＿SQ)

     if (MORE ＿ JUMPS in MOVE ＿ STAUS) *then*

     CONTINUE＿THE＿JUMP (PLAYER,NEW＿SQ)

     if NO＿KING (PLAYER) and MOVES＿LEFT (OPPONENT)
      then
        write (LEGAL＿MOVE＿MSG) for PLAYER
        write (MAKE ＿ MOVE ＿ MSG) for OPPONENT
        swap (PLAYER, OPPONENT)
    else
        write (WINNING＿MSG) for PLAYER
        write (LOSING＿MSG) for OPPONENT
        GAME＿OVER := TRUE
  else
     write (ILLEGAL ＿ MOVE ＿ MSG) for PLAYER

until GAME＿OVER

Although P_2 is in their own notation, Dorothy can now completely formalize P_2 into P_3, which is written in PASCAL (Example 3.1).

Example 3.1 P_3 (Formalized Version of Main Program)

```
BEGIN (* KRIEGSPIELREFEREE *)

    INITBOARD;
    INITBLACKMOVES;
    INITREDMOVES;

    PLAYER   := BLACK;
    OPPONENT := RED;

    SENDMESSAGE(PLAYER,   WELCOMEPLAYER);
    SENDMESSAGE(OPPONENT, WELCOMEOPPONENT);

    GAMEOVER := FALSE;

    REPEAT

        GETMOVE(PLAYER, OLDSQ, NEWSQ);

        EVALUATEMOVE(PLAYER, OLDSQ, NEWSQ, MOVESTATUS);

        IF LEGALMOVE IN MOVESTATUS THEN
            BEGIN

                UPDATEBOARD(PLAYER, OLDSQ, NEWSQ);

                IF MOREJUMPS IN MOVESTATUS THEN
                    CONTINUEJUMP(PLAYER, NEWSQ);

                    IF NOKING(PLAYER) AND MOVESLEFT(OPPONENT) THEN
                        BEGIN
                            SENDMESSAGE(PLAYER,   LEGALMOVEMADE);
                            SENDMESSAGE(OPPONENT, MAKEMOVE);
                            SWAP(PLAYER, OPPONENT)
                        END

                    ELSE
                        BEGIN
                            SENDMESSAGE(PLAYER,   VICTORY);
                            SENDMESSAGE(OPPONENT, DEFEAT);
                            GAMEOVER := TRUE
                        END

            END

        ELSE
            SENDMESSAGE(PLAYER, TRYAGAIN)

    UNTIL GAMEOVER

END. (* KRIEGSPIELREFEREE *)
```

The Remaining Functions and Subprograms

Now Dorothy takes over the task of specifying each subprogram. Since they are quite straightforward, we will not elaborate on each. We will describe one subprogram to give the reader a feel for operating on the board.

As the sample subprogram, we choose EVALUATEMOVE. This subroutine takes three arguments: PLAYER, SQ1, and SQ2. It returns the values of the move status flags.

For a legal move, the following conditions must be met:

1. The moving player must have a piece on SQ1.
2. SQ2 must be a left or right adjacent square.
3. SQ2 must be vacant.
4. If the move is a jump, the intervening square must contain an opponent's piece.
5. If a jump exists for the moving player, the move must not be a nonjump.

The path (left or right) and type of move is determined by GETPATHTYPE. NOJUMPS determines whether a player has a jump, and JUMPISLEGAL determines whether a jump is legal.

One important point must be made. Using the top-down approach, the main program has been so carefully defined and structured that all the procedures cannot be written *independently*. Any subprograms that fit their required definitions for the main program will suffice.

The complete, final program is comprised of the main program and the declaration of all subprograms (see Example 3.2). The reader should go over the main program and subprograms to be satisfied that they work correctly. The reader may have observed several ways of "speeding up" the Kriegspiel program. Efficiency was not a major design criterion in our development, although it could have been. Can you propose several changes to make the program more efficient?

The Real Story of Dorothy and Irene

The above story, with a suitable change of names and places, is by and large accurate. In fact, in writing this chapter, we tried to follow the top-down approach *exactly*. In fairness to you, the reader, we would like to summarize what actually happened.

First, the inputs, outputs, and condition-action mapping underwent many minor revisions as a result of writing the actual program. We consider this a mistake on our part for not meticulously thinking ahead.

Second, we found it important to include a move status value for a legal (or nonlegal) jump in the subroutine to evaluate a legal move. In lower level modules, we found that such a value was needed. We consider this a serious flaw, for the main program underwent a change that was not anticipated in the original development as given in the text.

Finally, there were debates on the actual kind of error checking performed by the program. This is a difficult area, and the influence of PASCAL had some effect on our final decisions.

In parting, we make several comments:

1. We strongly believe in the top-down approach.
2. With any approach, we cannot overemphasize the importance of thinking, and especially, thinking before any code is written.
3. Looking at the final program, which we believe is first-rate, we have noticed a somewhat different, and better, organization. We leave this little exercise to you.

So be it.

Example 3.2 Final Program for Kriegspiel Checkers

```
(*
   ** PROGRAM TITLE:    KRIEGSPIEL CHECKERS
   ** WRITTEN BY:       DR.  IRENE B.  MALCOLM AND DOROTHY E.  CLARK
   ** DATE WRITTEN:     JANUARY, 1979
   ** WRITTEN FOR:      COMMISSION ON RECREATIONAL ACTIVIITIES,
   **                   STATE OF ATAD
   **
   **
   ** PROGRAM INTENT:
   **
   **    THIS PROGRAM ACTS AS THE REFEREE FOR THE GAME OF
   **    KRIEGSPIEL CHECKERS AS DEFINED IN THE STATE OF ATAD.
   **    THE INPUT TO THIS PROGRAM CONSISTS OF A SERIES OF
   **    MOVES TAKEN FROM TWO INTERACTIVE TERMINALS.   THE
   **    OUTPUT IS THE SEQUENCE OF MESSAGES INFORMING THE
   **    PLAYERS OF THE CURRENT STATUS OF THE GAME.
   **
   **    THERE ARE TWO MAJOR DATA STRUCTURES:
   **
   **    (1)  BOARD GIVES THE STATUS OF EACH OF THE 32 SQUARES,
   **         I.E. WHETHER THE SQUARE IS OCCUPIED BY A RED PIECE,
   **         A BLACK PIECE, OR NEITHER (VACANT).
   **
   **    (2)  BLACKMOVES (OR REDMOVES) INDICATES THE POSSIBLE
   **         PATHS THAT A BLACK (OR RED) PIECE CAN TAKE FROM A
   **         GIVEN STARTING SQUARE.   THERE ARE 32 ENTRIES,
   **         CORRESPONDING TO THE 32 SQUARES ON THE BOARD, AND 4
   **         VALUES PER ENTRY, CORRESPONDING TO THE 4 POSSIBLE
   **         PATHS FROM A GIVEN SQUARE.   THE PATHS ARE DEFINED AS:
   **
   **             LEFT-ADJACENT SQUARE    (LEFTADJ)
   **             RIGHT-ADJACENT SQUARE   (RIGHTADJ)
   **             LEFT-JUMP SQUARE        (LEFTJMP)
   **             RIGHT-JUMP SQUARE       (RIGHTJMP)
   **
   **         IF BOARD POSITIONS DO NOT EXIST ALONG ANY OF
   **         THE 4 PATHS, THOSE POSITIONS ARE MARKED AS NULL (NULLSQ).
   **
   **
   ** INPUT AND OUTPUT FILES:
   **
   **    BLACKSTERMINAL   I/O DEVICE FOR PLAYER WITH BLACK PIECES
   **    REDSTERMINAL     I/O DEVICE FOR PLAYER WITH RED PIECES
   **
   **
   ** DICTIONARY OF GLOBAL CONSTANTS AND VARIABLES:
   **
   **    NUMSQS       INDICATES THE NUMBER OF SQUARES ON THE BOARD
   **    NULLSQ       INDICATES AN ILLEGAL SQUARE
   **    BOARD        A VARIALE ARRAY THAT CONTAINS THE CURRENT
   **                 STATE OF ALL SQUARES (SEE ABOVE).   A SQUARE
   **                 MAY CONTAIN A BLACKPIECE, REDPIECE, OR BE VACANT.
   **    BLACKMOVES   INDICATES THE PATHS FOR THE PLAYER WITH BLACK PIECES
   **    REDMOVES     INDICATES THE PATHS FOR THE PLAYER WITH RED PIECES
*)
```

Example 3.2 Final Program (Cont'd)

```
PROGRAM KRIEGSPIELREFEREE( (* BETWEEN *) BLACKSTERMINAL,
                           (* AND *)     REDSTERMINAL   );

CONST
        NUMSQS = 32;
        NULLSQ = 0;

TYPE
        PARTICIPANT = (BLACK, RED);

        SQNUM       = 1..NUMSQS;
        SQCONTENTS = (BLACKPIECE, REDPIECE, VACANT);

        PATH        = (LEFTADJ, RIGHTADJ, LEFTJMP, RIGHTJMP);
        DESTINATION = 0..NUMSQS;
        POSSIBLEMOVES = ARRAY [SQNUM, PATH] OF DESTINATION;

        STATUS = SET OF (LEGALMOVE, JUMPMOVE, MOREJUMPS, JUMPAVAILABLE);

        MESSAGE = (WELCOMEPLAYER,    WELCOMEOPPONENT, MAKEMOVE,
                   LEGALMOVEMADE,    TRYAGAIN,        DEFEAT,
                   VICTORY,          MUSTJUMP,        JUMPAGAIN,
                   ILLEGALJUMPCON,   PIECETAKEN,      BADSEPARATOR,
                   NONNUMERICCHAR,   SQOUTOFRANGE);

        TERMINAL    = FILE OF CHAR;
        INPUTBUFFER = ARRAY [1..5] OF CHAR;

VAR
        BLACKSTERMINAL,
        REDSTERMINAL   : TERMINAL;

        BOARD: ARRAY [SQNUM] OF SQCONTENTS;

        BLACKMOVES,
        REDMOVES   : POSSIBLEMOVES;

        PLAYER,
        OPPONENT: PARTICIPANT;

        MOVESTATUS: STATUS;

        GAMEOVER: BOOLEAN;

        OLDSQ,
        NEWSQ : SQNUM;
```

Example 3.2 Final Program (Cont'd)

```
PROCEDURE INITBOARD;

CONST
      FIRSTBLACKSQ =  1;
      LASTBLACKSQ  = 12;

      FIRSTVACANTSQ = 13;
      LASTVACANTSQ  = 20;

      FIRSTREDSQ = 21;
      LASTREDSQ  = 32;

VAR
    SQ: SQNUM;


BEGIN (* INITBOARD *)

   FOR SQ := FIRSTBLACKSQ TO LASTBLACKSQ DO
      BOARD[SQ] := BLACKPIECE;

   FOR SQ := FIRSTVACANTSQ TO LASTVACANTSQ DO
      BOARD[SQ] := VACANT;

   FOR SQ := FIRSTREDSQ TO LASTREDSQ DO
      BOARD[SQ] := REDPIECE

END; (* INITBOARD *)
```

Example 3.2 Final Program (Cont'd)

```
PROCEDURE INITBLACKMOVES;

VAR
    SQ: SQNUM;


BEGIN (* INITBLACKMOVES *)

(* LEFT ADJACENT PATHS *)

    FOR SQ := 1 TO NUMSQS DO
        IF SQ IN [1, 2, 3, 4,  9, 10, 11, 12,  17, 18, 19, 20,  25, 26, 27, 28] THEN
            BLACKMOVES[SQ, LEFTADJ] := SQ + 4
        ELSE IF IN [6, 7, 8,  14, 15, 16,  22, 23, 24] THEN
            BLACKMOVES[SQ, LEFTADJ] := SQ + 3
        ELSE
            BLACKMOVES[SQ, LEFTADJ] := NULLSQ;

(* RIGHT ADJACENT PATHS *)

    FOR SQ := 1 TO NUMSQS DO
        IF SQ IN [1, 2, 3,  9, 10, 11,  17, 18, 19,  25, 26, 27] THEN
            BLACKMOVES[SQ, RIGHTADJ] := SQ + 5
        ELSE IF SQ IN [5, 6, 7, 8,  13, 14, 15, 16,  21, 22, 23, 24] THEN
            BLACKMOVES[SQ, RIGHTADJ] := SQ + 4
        ELSE
            BLACKMOVES[SQ, RIGHTADJ] := NULLSQ;

(* LEFT JUMP PATHS *)

    FOR SQ := 1 TO NUMSQS DO
        IF SQ IN [ 2,  3,  4,.  6,  7,  8,  10, 11, 12,
                  14, 15, 16,  18, 19, 20,  22, 23, 24 ] THEN
            BLACKMOVES[SQ, LEFTJMP] := SQ + 7
        ELSE
            BLACKMOVES[SQ, LEFTJMP] := NULLSQ;

(* RIGHT JUMP PATHS *)

    FOR SQ := 1 TO NUMSQS DO
        IF SQ IN [ 1,  2,  3,   5,  6,  7,   9, 10, 11,
                  13, 14, 15,  17, 18, 19,  22, 23, 24 ] THEN
            BLACKMOVES[SQ, RIGHTJMP] := SQ + 9
        ELSE
            BLACKMOVES[SQ, RIGHTJMP] := NULLSQ

END; (* INITBLACKMOVES *)
```

Example 3.2 Final Program (Cont'd)

```
PROCEDURE INITREDMOVES;

VAR
    SQ: SQNUM;


BEGIN (* INITREDMOVES *)

(* LEFT ADJACENT PATHS *)

    FOR SQ := 1 TO NUMSQS DO
        IF SQ IN [6,7,8,  14,15,16,  22,23,24,  30,31,32] THEN
            REDMOVES[SQ, LEFTADJ] := SQ - 5
        ELSE IF SQ IN [9,10,11,12,  17,18,19,20,  25,26,27,28] THEN
            REDMOVES[SQ, LEFTADJ] := SQ - 4
        ELSE
            REDMOVES[SQ, LEFTADJ] := NULLSQ;

(* RIGHT ADJACENT PATHS *)

    FOR SQ := 1 TO NUMSQS DO
        IF SQ IN [5,6,7,8,  13,14,15,16,  21,22,23,24,  29,30,31,32] THEN
            REDMOVES[SQ, RIGHTADJ] := SQ - 4
        ELSE IF SQ IN [9,10,11,  17,18,19,  25,26,27] THEN
            REDMOVES[SQ, RIGHTADJ] := SQ - 3
        ELSE
            REDMOVES[SQ, RIGHTADJ] := NULLSQ;

(* LEFT JUMP PATHS *)

    FOR SQ := 1 TO NUMSQS DO
        IF SQ IN [10,11,12,  14,15,16,  18,19,20,
                  22,23,24,  26,27,28,  30,31,32 ] THEN
            REDMOVES[SQ, LEFTJMP] := SQ - 9
        ELSE
            REDMOVES[SQ, LEFTJMP] := NULLSQ;

(* RIGHT JUMP PATHS *)

    FOR SQ := 1 TO NUMSQS DO
        IF SQ IN [ 9,10,11,  13,14,15,  17,18,19,
                  21,22,23,  25,26,27,  29,30,31 ] THEN
            REDMOVES[SQ, RIGHTJMP] := SQ - 7
        ELSE
            REDMOVES[SQ, RIGHTJMP] := NULLSQ

END; (* INITREDMOVES *)
```

Example 3.2 Final Program (Cont'd)

```
PROCEDURE SENDMESSAGE( (* TO *)                    PLAYER   : PARTICIPANT;
                      (* CORRESPONDING TO *) MESSAGEID: MESSAGE      );

VAR
    DEVICE: TERMINAL;


BEGIN (* SENDMESSAGE *)

    IF PLAYER = BLACK
       THEN
           DEVICE := BLACKSTERMINAL
       ELSE
           DEVICE := REDSTERMINAL;

    REWRITE(DEVICE);

    WRITELN(DEVICE);

    CASE MESSAGEID OF

       WELCOMEPLAYER:
           BEGIN
               WRITELN(DEVICE, 'WELCOME TO KRIEGSPIEL CHECKERS');
               WRITELN(DEVICE, 'ENTER YOUR FIRST MOVE');
               WRITELN(DEVICE, 'XX XX')
           END;

       WELCOMEOPPONENT:
           BEGIN
               WRITELN(DEVICE, 'WELCOME TO KRIEGSPIEL CHECKERS');
               WRITELN(DEVICE, 'YOUR OPPONENT WILL MAKE THE FIRST MOVE')
           END;

       MAKEMOVE:
           BEGIN
               WRITELN(DEVICE, 'IT IS YOUR TURN TO MOVE');
               WRITELN(DEVICE, 'XX XX')
           END;

       LEGALMOVEMADE:
           BEGIN
               WRITELN(DEVICE, 'YOU HAVE COMPLETED A LEGAL MOVE AND');
               WRITELN(DEVICE, 'YOUR OPPONENT HAS BEEN ASKED TO MOVE')
           END;

       TRYAGAIN:
           BEGIN
               WRITELN(DEVICE, 'TRY AGAIN');
               WRITELN(DEVICE, 'XX XX')
           END;
```

Example 3.2 Final Program (Cont'd)

```
DEFAT:
   WRITELN(DEVICE, 'SORRY...YOUR OPPONENT HAS WON THE GAME!!!');

VICTORY:
   WRITELN(DEVICE, 'CONGRATULATIONS...YOU HAVE WON THE GAME!!!');

MUSTJUMP:
   WRITELN(DEVICE, 'A JUMP IS AVAILABLE AND YOU MUST TAKE IT');

JUMPAGAIN:
   BEGIN
      WRITELN(DEVICE, 'YOUR JUMP MUST BE CONTINUED');
      WRITELN(DEVICE, 'ENTER JUMP SQUARE');
      WRITELN(DEVICE, 'XX')
   END;

ILLEGALJUMPCON:
   WRITELN(DEVICE, 'ILLEGAL JUMP CONTINUATION');

PIECETAKEN:
   WRITE(DEVICE, 'PIECE TAKEN FROM SQUARE ');

BADESEPARATOR:
   WRITELN(DEVICE, 'NO SPACE OR COMMA BETWEEN SQUARES');

NONNUMERICCHAR:
   WRITELN(DEVICE, 'NONNUMERIC CHARACTERS IN SQUARE');

SQOUTOFRANGE:
   WRITELN(DEVICE, 'SQUARE NUMBER OUT OF RANGE')

END (* CASE *)

END; (* SENDMESSAGE *)
```

Example 3.2 Final Program (Cont'd)

```
PROCEDURE READMOVE( (* FROM *) VAR PLAYERSTERMINAL: TERMINAL;
                                   EXPECTEDCHARS:   INTEGER;
                    (* INTO *) VAR BUFFER:          INPUTBUFFER);

CONST
      BLANK = ' ';

VAR
    CHARPOS: INTEGER;


BEGIN (* READMOVE *)

   FOR CHARPOS := 1 TO EXPECTEDCHARS DO
      BUFFER[CHARPOS] := BLANK;

   RESET(PLAYERSTERMINAL);

   CHARPOS := 1;

   WHILE NOT(EOLN(PLAYERSTERMINAL)) AND (CHARPOS <= EXPECTEDCHARS) DO
      BEGIN
         READ(PLAYERSTERMINAL, BUFFER[CHARPOS]);
         CHARPOS := CHARPOS + 1
      END;

   READLN(PLAYERSTERMINAL)

END; (* READMOVE *)
```

Example 3.2 Final Program (Cont'd)

```
FUNCTION DIGIT(CHARACTER: CHAR): INTEGER;
BEGIN (* DIGIT *)
   DIGIT := ORD(CHARACTER) - ORD('O')
END; (* DIGIT *)
```

Example 3.2 Final Program (Cont'd)

```
PROCEDURE GETSQUARE( (* FROM *)              BUFFER:    INPUTBUFFER;
                     (* STARTING AT *)       STARTPOS:  INTEGER;
                     (* FOR *)               PLAYER:    PARTICIPANT;
                     (* RETURNING *)     VAR SQ:        SQNUM;
                                         VAR ERROR:     BOOLEAN);


CONST
      BLANK = ' ';

VAR
     VALIDCHARS: SET OF CHAR;

     INPUTNUM: INTEGER;


BEGIN (* GETSQUARE *)

   VALIDCHARS := ['0'..'9', BLANK];

   IF NOT((BUFFER[STARTPOS]   IN  VALIDCHARS)  AND
          (BUFFER[STARTPOS+1] IN VALIDCHARS)) THEN
      BEGIN
         ERROR := TRUE;
         SENDMESSAGE(PLAYER, NONNUMERICCHAR)
      END

   ELSE
      BEGIN

         IF BUFFER[STARTPOS] <> BLANK
            THEN
               INPUTNUM := DIGIT(BUFFER[STARTPOS])
            ELSE
               INPUTNUM := 0;

         IF BUFFER[STARTPOS+1] <> BLANK
            THEN
               INPUTNUM := INPUTNUM*10 + DIGIT(BUFFER[STARTPOS+1]);

         IF (INPUTNUM < 1) OR (INPUTNUM > NUMSQS) THEN
            BEGIN
               ERROR := TRUE;
               SENDMESSAGE(PLAYER, SQOUTOFRANGE)
            END

         ELSE
            BEGIN
               ERROR := FALSE;
               SQ    := INPUTNUM
            END

      END

END; (* GETSQUARE *)
```

Example 3.2 Final Program (Cont'd)

```
PROCEDURE GETMOVE( (* FROM *)          PLAYER: PARTICIPANT;
                   (* RETURNING *) VAR OLDSQ,
                                       NEWSQ : SQNUM);

CONST
      BLANK = ' ';
      COMMA = ',';

      EXPECTEDCHARS = 5;
      FIRSTSQPOS    = 1;
      SECONDSQPOS   = 4;

VAR
    BUFFER: INPUTBUFFER;

    ERROR: BOOLEAN;


BEGIN (* GETMOVE *)

    REPEAT

        IF PLAYER = BLACK
           THEN
               READMOVE(BLACKSTERMINAL, EXPECTEDCHARS, BUFFER)
           ELSE
               READMOVE(REDSTERMINAL, EXPECTEDCHARS, BUFFER);

        GETSQUARE(BUFFER, FIRSTSQPOS, PLAYER, OLDSQ, ERROR);

        IF NOT ERROR
           THEN
               IF (BUFFER[3] = BLANK) OR (BUFFER[3] = COMMA)
                  THEN
                      GETSQUARE(BUFFER, SECONDSQPOS, PLAYER, NEWSQ, ERROR)
                  ELSE
                      BEGIN
                          SENDMESSAGE(PLAYER, BADSEPARATOR);
                          ERROR := TRUE
                      END;

        IF ERROR THEN
           SENDMESSAGE(PLAYER, TRYAGAIN)

    UNTIL NOT ERROR

END; (* GETMOVE *)
```

Example 3.2 Final Program (Cont'd)

```
PROCEDURE GETPATHTYPE( (* FOR *)          PLAYER:      PARTICIPANT;
                       (* FROM *)         OLDSQ,
                       (* TO *)           NEWSQ :      SQNUM;
                       (* RETURNING *) VAR PATHCHOSEN: PATH;
                                       VAR ERROR:     BOOLEAN);

VAR
    THISPATH: PATH;


BEGIN (* GETPATHTYPE *)

   ERROR := TRUE;

   FOR THISPATH := LEFTADJ TO RIGHTJMP DO

      CASE PLAYER OF

          BLACK:
             IF BLACKMOVES[OLDSQ, THISPATH] = NEWSQ THEN
                BEGIN
                   PATHCHOSEN := THISPATH;
                   ERROR      := FALSE
                END;

          RED:
             IF REDMOVES[OLDSQ, THISPATH] = NEWSQ THEN
                BEGIN
                   PATHCHOSEN := THISPATH;
                   ERROR      := FALSE
                END

      END (* CASE *)

END; (* GETPATHTYPE *)
```

Example 3.2 Final Program (Cont'd)

```
FUNCTION JUMPPATHFREE( (* FOR *)  PLAYER: PARTICIPANT;
                      (* FROM *) OLDSQ:  SQNUM      ): BOOLEAN;

VAR
    OPPONENTSPIECE: BLACKPIECE..REDPIECE;
    MOVES:          POSSIBLEMOVES;
    FREEPATHFOUND:  BOOLEAN;

BEGIN (* JUMPPATHFREE *)

    IF PLAYER = BLACK THEN
       BEGIN
          OPPONENTSPIECE := REDPIECE;
          MOVES          := BLACKMOVES
       END
    ELSE
       BEGIN
          OPPONENTSPIECE := BLACKPIECE;
          MOVES          := REDMOVES
       END;

    FREEPATHFOUND := FALSE;

    IF MOVES[OLDSQ, LEFTJMP] <> NULLSQ
       THEN
          IF (BOARD[MOVES[OLDSQ, LEFTJMP]] = VACANT)          AND
             (BOARD[MOVES[OLDSQ, LEFTADJ]] = OPPONENTSPIECE) THEN
                FREEPATHFOUND := TRUE;

    IF MOVES[OLDSQ, RIGHTJMP] <> NULLSQ
       THEN
          IF (BOARD[MOVES[OLDSQ, RIGHTJMP]] = VACANT)          AND
             (BOARD[MOVES[OLDSQ, RIGHTADJ]] = OPPONENTSPIECE) THEN
                FREEPATHFOUND := TRUE;

    JUMPPATHFREE := FREEPATHFOUND

END; (* JUMPPATHFREE *)
```

Example 3.2 Final Program (Cont'd)

```
FUNCTION NOJUMPS( (* FOR *) PLAYER: PARTICIPANT): BOOLEAN;

VAR
    THISSQNUM: 0..NUMSQS;
    JUMPFOUND: BOOLEAN;

BEGIN (* NOJUMPS *)

    THISSQNUM := 0;
    JUMPFOUND := FALSE;

    REPEAT

        THISSQNUM := THISSQNUM + 1;

        CASE PLAYER OF

            BLACK:
                IF BOARD[THISSQNUM] = BLACKPIECE
                    THEN
                        JUMPFOUND := JUMPPATHFREE(PLAYER, THISSQNUM);

                RED:
                    IF BOARD[THISSQNUM] = REDPIECE
                        THEN
                            JUMPFOUND := JUMPPATHFREE(PLAYER, THISSQNUM)

            END (* CASE *)

    UNTIL JUMPFOUND OR (THISSQNUM = NUMSQS);

    NOJUMPS := NOT JUMPFOUND

END; (* NOJUMPS *)
```

Example 3.2 Final Program (Cont'd)

```
FUNCTION JUMPISLEGAL( (* FOR *)    PLAYER:      PARTICIPANT;
                      (* FROM *)   OLDSQ:       SQNUM;
                      (* ALONG *)  PATHCHOSEN:  PATH   ): BOOLEAN;

VAR
    ADJACENTPATH:     PATH;
    OPPONENT:         PARTICIPANT;
    OPPONENTSPIECE:   BLACKPIECE..REDPIECE;
    OPPONENTSTERM:    TERMINAL;
    SQBETWEEN:        SQNUM;


BEGIN (* JUMPISLEGAL *)

   IF PATHCHOSEN = LEFTJMP
      THEN
         ADJACENTPATH := LEFTADJ
      ELSE
         ADJACENTPATH := RIGHTADJ;

   CASE PLAYER OF

   BLACK:
      BEGIN
         OPPONENT        := RED;
         OPPONENTSPIECE  := REDPIECE;
         OPPONENTSTERM   := REDSTERMINAL;
         SQBETWEEN       := BLACKMOVES[OLDSQ, ADJACENTPATH]
      END;

   RED:
      BEGIN
         OPPONENT        := BLACK;
         OPPONENTSPIECE  := BLACKPIECE;
         OPPONENTSTERM   := BLACKSTERMINAL;
         SQBETWEEN       := REDMOVES[OLDSQ, ADJACENTPATH]
      END

   END; (* CASE *)

   IF BOARD[SQBETWEEN] = OPPONENTSPIECE THEN
      BEGIN
         JUMPISLEGAL := TRUE;
         SENDMESSAGE(OPPONENT, PIECETAKEN);
         WRITELN(OPPONENTSTERM, SQBETWEEN)
      END

   ELSE
      JUMPISLEGAL := FALSE

END; (* JUMPISLEGAL *)
```

Example 3.2 Final Program (Cont'd)

```
PROCEDURE EVALUATEMOVE( (* GIVEN BY *)        PLAYER:      PARTICIPANT;
                       (* FROM *)             OLDSQ,
                       (* TO *)               NEWSQ :      SQNUM;
                       (* RETURNING *) VAR MOVESTATUS: STATUS);

VAR
    PLAYERSPIECE: BLACKPIECE..REDPIECE;
    PATHCHOSEN:   PATH;
    ERROR:        BOOLEAN;


BEGIN (* EVALUATEMOVE *)

   IF PLAYER = BLACK
      THEN
         PLAYERSPIECE := BLACKPIECE
      ELSE
         PLAYERSPIECE := REDPIECE;

   MOVESTATUS := [];

   IF (BOARD[OLDSQ] = PLAYERSPIECE) AND (BOARD[NEWSQ] = VACANT) THEN
      BEGIN

         GETPATHTYPE(PLAYER, OLDSQ, NEWSQ, PATHCHOSEN, ERROR);

         IF NOT ERROR THEN
            CASE PATHCHOSEN OF

               LEFTADJ, RIGHTADJ:
                  IF NOJUMPS(PLAYER)
                     THEN
                        MOVESTATUS := [LEGALMOVE]
                     ELSE
                        MOVESTATUS := [JUMPAVAILABLE];

               LEFTJMP, RIGHTJMP:
                  IF JUMPISLEGAL(PLAYER, OLDSQ, PATHCHOSEN) THEN
                     BEGIN

                        MOVESTATUS := [LEGALMOVE, JUMPMOVE];

                        IF JUMPPATHFREE(PLAYER, NEWSQ)
                           THEN
                              MOVESTATUS := MOVESTATUS + [MOREJUMPS]

                     END (* IF *)

            END (* CASE *)

      END (* IF *)

END; (* EVALUATEMOVE *)
```

Example 3.2 Final Program (Cont'd)

```
PROCEDURE UPDATEBOARD( (* FOR *)              PLAYER: PARTICIPANT;
                      (* MOVING FROM *) OLDSQ,
                      (* TO *)              NEWSQ : SQNUM);

BEGIN (* UPDATEBOARD *)

   BOARD[NEWSQ] := BOARD[OLDSQ];
   BOARD[OLDSQ] := VACANT;

   CASE PLAYER OF

      BLACK:
         IF BLACKMOVES[OLDSQ, LEFTJMP] = NEWSQ
            THEN
               BOARD[BLACKMOVES[OLDSQ, LEFTADJ]]  := VACANT

         ELSE IF BLACKMOVES[OLDSQ, RIGHTJMP] = NEWSQ
            THEN
               BOARD[BLACKMOVES[OLDSQ, RIGHTADJ]] := VACANT;

      RED:
         IF REDMOVES[OLDSQ, LEFTJMP] = NEWSQ
            THEN
               BOARD[REDMOVES[OLDSQ, LEFTADJ]]  := VACANT

         ELSE IF REDMOVES[OLDSQ, RIGHTJMP] = NEWSQ
            THEN
               BOARD[REDMOVES[OLDSQ, RIGHTADJ]] := VACANT

   END (* CASE *)

END; (* UPDATEBOARD *)
```

Example 3.2 Final Program (Cont'd)

```
PROCEDURE GETJUMPMOVE( (* FROM *)                    PLAYER: PARTICIPANT;
                       (* RETURNING *) VAR NEWSQ:   SQNUM      );

CONST
      BLANK        = ' ';
      EXPECTEDCHARS = 2;
      SQSTARTPOS    = 1;

VAR
    BUFFER: INPUTBUFFER;

    ERROR: BOOLEAN;

BEGIN (* GETJUMPMOVE *)

   REPEAT

      IF PLAYER = BLACK
         THEN
            READMOVE(BLACKSTERMINAL, EXPECTEDCHARS, BUFFER)
         ELSE
            READMOVE(REDSTERMINAL, EXPECTEDCHARS, BUFFER);

      GETSQUARE(BUFFER, SQSTARTPOS, PLAYER, NEWSQ, ERROR);

      IF ERROR THEN
         SENDMESSAGE(PLAYER, TRYAGAIN)

   UNTIL NOT ERROR

END; (* GETJUMPMOVE *)
```

Example 3.2 Final Program (Cont'd)

```
PROCEDURE CONTINUEJUMP( (* FOR *)  PLAYER:   PARTICIPANT;
                       (* FROM *) STARTSQ: SQNUM        );

VAR
    OLDSQ,
    NEWSQ : SQNUM;

    MOVESTATUS: STATUS;


BEGIN (* CONTINUEJUMP *)

   OLDSQ := STARTSQ;

   REPEAT

      SENDMESSAGE(PLAYER, JUMPAGAIN);

      REPEAT

         GETJUMPMOVE(PLAYER, NEWSQ);

         EVALUATEMOVE(PLAYER, OLDSQ, NEWSQ, MOVESTATUS);

         IF NOT(JUMPMOVE IN MOVESTATUS) THEN
            BEGIN
               SENDMESSAGE(PLAYER, ILLEGALJUMPCON);
               SENDMESSAGE(PLAYER, TRYAGAIN)
            END

      UNTIL JUMPMOVE IN MOVESTATUS;

      UPDATEBOARD(PLAYER, OLDSQ, NEWSQ);

      OLDSQ := NEWSQ

   UNTIL NOT(MOREJUMPS IN MOVESTATUS)

END; (* CONTINUEJUMP *)
```

Example 3.2 Final Program (Cont'd)

```
FUNCTION NOKING( (* FOR *) PLAYER: PARTICIPANT): BOOLEAN;

VAR
    PLAYERSPIECE: BLACKPIECE..REDPIECE;
    LASTROW:     SET OF SQCONTENTS;


BEGIN (* NOKING *)

   CASE PLAYER OF

      BLACK:
         BEGIN
            PLAYERSPIECE := BLACKPIECE;
            LASTROW      := [BOARD[29], BOARD[30],
                            BOARD[31], BOARD[32]]
         END;

      RED:
         BEGIN
            PLAYERSPIECE := REDPIECE;
            LASTROW      := [BOARD[1], BOARD[2],
                            BOARD[3], BOARD[4]]
         END

   END; (* CASE *)

   IF PLAYERSPIECE IN LASTROW
      THEN
         NOKING := FALSE
      ELSE
         NOKING := TRUE

END; (* NOKING *)
```

Example 3.2 Final Program (Cont'd)

```
FUNCTION PATHFREE( (* FOR *)  PLAYER: PARTICIPANT;
                   (* FROM *) OLDSQ:  SQNUM        ): BOOLEAN;

VAR
    FREEPATHFOUND: BOOLEAN;
    MOVES:         POSSIBLEMOVES;


BEGIN (* PATHFREE *)

   IF PLAYER = BLACK
      THEN
         MOVES := BLACKMOVES
      ELSE
         MOVES := REDMOVES;

   FREEPATHFOUND := FALSE;

   IF MOVES[OLDSQ, LEFTADJ] <> NULLSQ
      THEN
         IF BOARD[MOVES[OLDSQ, LEFTADJ]] = VACANT THEN
            FREEPATHFOUND := TRUE;

   IF MOVES[OLDSQ, RIGHTADJ] <> NULLSQ
      THEN
         IF BOARD[MOVES[OLDSQ, RIGHTADJ]] = VACANT THEN
            FREEPATHFOUND := TRUE;

   IF NOT FREEPATHFOUND
      THEN
         FREEPATHFOUND := JUMPPATHFREE(PLAYER, OLDSQ);

   PATHFREE := FREEPATHFOUND

END; (* PATHFREE *)
```

Example 3.2 Final Program (Cont'd)

```
FUNCTION MOVESLEFT( (* FOR *) PLAYER: PARTICIPANT): BOOLEAN;

VAR
    THISSQNUM: 0..NUMSQS;
    MOVEFOUND: BOOLEAN;

BEGIN (* MOVESLEFT *)

    THISSQNUM := 0;
    MOVEFOUND := FALSE;

    REPEAT

        THISSQNUM := THISSQNUM + 1;

        CASE PLAYER OF

            BLACK:
                IF BOARD[THISSQNUM] = BLACKPIECE
                    THEN
                        MOVEFOUND := PATHFREE(PLAYER, THISSQNUM);

            RED:
                IF BOARD[SQUARENUM] = REDPIECE
                    THEN
                        MOVEFOUND := PATHFREE(PLAYER, THISSQNUM)

        END (* CASE *)

    UNTIL MOVEFOUND OR (THISSQNUM = NUMSQS);

    MOVESLEFT := MOVEFOUND

END; (* MOVESLEFT *)
```

```
PROCEDURE SWAP(VAR PLAYER, (* AND *) OPPONENT: PARTICIPANT);

VAR
    OLDPLAYER: PARTICIPANT;

BEGIN (* SWAP *)

    OLDPLAYER := PLAYER;
    PLAYER    := OPPONENT;
    OPPONENT  := OLDPLAYER

END; (* SWAP *)
```

Example 3.2 Final Program (Cont'd)

```
BEGIN (* KRIEGSPIELREFEREE *)

    INITBOARD;
    INITBLACKMOVES;
    INITREDMOVES;

    PLAYER   := BLACK;
    OPPONENT := RED;

    SENDMESSAGE(PLAYER,   WELCOMEPLAYER);
    SENDMESSAGE(OPPONENT, WELCOMEOPPONENT);

    GAMEOVER := FALSE;

    REPEAT

        GETMOVE(PLAYER, OLDSQ, NEWSQ);

        EVALUATEMOVE(PLAYER, OLDSQ, NEWSQ, MOVESTATUS);

        IF LEGALMOVE IN MOVESTATUS THEN
            BEGIN

                UPDATEBOARD(PLAYER, OLDSQ, NEWSQ);

                IF MOREJUMPS IN MOVESTATUS THEN
                    CONTINUEJUMP(PLAYER, NEWSQ);

                    IF NOKING(PLAYER) AND MOVESLEFT(OPPONENT) THEN
                        BEGIN
                            SENDMESSAGE(PLAYER,   LEGALMOVEMADE);
                            SENDMESSAGE(OPPONENT, MAKEMOVE);
                            SWAP(PLAYER, OPPONENT)
                        END

                    ELSE
                        BEGIN
                            SENDMESSAGE(PLAYER,   VICTORY);
                            SENDMESSAGE(OPPONENT, DEFEAT);
                            GAMEOVER := TRUE
                        END

            END

        ELSE
            SENDMESSAGE(PLAYER, TRYAGAIN)

    UNTIL GAMEOVER

END. (* KRIEGSPIELREFEREE *)
```

EXERCISES

Exercise 3.1   (Programming Proverbs)
List three ways in which Irene and Dorothy followed the proverb, "Don't Leave the Reader in the Dust."

Exercise 3.2   (Programming Approaches)
Write a short position paper comparing the "top-down" approach with the "systems analyst" approach of Chapter 2.

Exercise 3.3   (The Input/Output Mapping)
Develop an alternative to the condition-action list method for expressing how a program is to map input situations to output responses. Consider a decision table approach.

Exercise 3.4   (Program Levels)
Draw a complete tree in the form of Fig. 3.2 to illustrate the levels of the Kriegspiel program.

Exercise 3.5   (Writing the Levels of a Given Program)
Write a sequence of levels that might have been used to generate the program in the prettyprint proverb.

Exercise 3.6   (Program Modification)
Modify the Kriegspiel program to accept moves in a completely free format, that is, without requiring column placement of the two squares.

Exercise 3.7   (Program Critique)
List five parts of the Kriegspiel program that, from a quality point of view, can be improved.

Exercise 3.8   (Speeding Up a Program)
Discuss five different ways for speeding up the Kriegspiel program. If you had to pick one way, which would cause the greatest speed-up?

Exercise 3.9   (Program Development)
Write both an informal and formal statement of the P_3 module "EVALUATEMOVE" for the Kriegspiel program.

Exercise 3.10   (Program Development)
Following the same specification and top-down development strategy as Irene's, present a complete program to solve the following problem:

Input: a sequence of characters representing the text of a letter. The text contains only alphabetic English words, blanks, commas, periods, and the special word "PP" denoting the beginning of a paragraph.

Output: 1. The number of words in the text.
2. The text given as input, printed according to the following format:
   a. The first line of each paragraph is to be indented five spaces and successive lines are to be left-adjusted. Lines are printed in units of 60 or fewer characters.
   b. One blank is to separate each word from the previous word, comma, or period.
   c. A word cannot be broken across lines.

Exercise 3.11 (Programming Pressure)
Will Irene take over Mr. Coleman's job?

CHAPTER FOUR
PROGRAM STANDARDS

"Any programmer who fails to comply with the standard naming, formatting or commenting conventions should be shot. If it so happens that it is inconvenient to shoot him, then he is to be politely requested to recode his program in adherence to the above standard."

Michael Spier [Ref. S1]

The PASCAL language has been with us for many years, yet the writing of high-quality PASCAL programs has remained a matter of personal style. The thrust of this chapter is to go beyond the "proverbs" and present some rigorous standards for the writing of PASCAL programs. Developing rigorous program standards is not easy, for the rules must be unambiguous, of sufficient merit so that a programmer will not be unduly stifled by their adoption, and ideally, machine testable. We have followed this chapter's program standards throughout this book.

The importance of developing such standards is clear. For managers, instructors, and programmers, there is a need to develop uniform rules so that everyone may more easily understand programs, a need to develop coding techniques that reduce the complexity of programs, and a need to control the entire software development effort.

We make no attempt here to encompass every feature of the PASCAL language. No standard can attempt to cover every aspect of a given programming problem. Nevertheless, the standards presented in this book should go a long way to promote quality programs. Furthermore, no attempt is made to consider the consequences if the adoption of standards results in the loss of efficiency. Too great a loss may be due cause for revocation of some standards.

GENERAL REQUIREMENTS

[GEN-1]   *Any violation of the program standards must be approved by someone appointed to enforce the standards.*

The rationale here is to allow exceptions to the program standards, but *only* if a responsible agent gives approval. It is critical that all program standards, unless revoked, be followed to the very last detail. The method for enforcing the standards is left to the particular instructor or manager.

[GEN-2]   *For each installation and for each application there should be an adopted set of standard user-defined names.*

The standard words should be chosen *before* coding. The following set of names is a very small sample of those that might be adopted for a PASCAL preprocessor:

SYMBOL	For atomic symbols
GETSYMBOL	For a subroutine to input symbols
SYMBOLLENGTH	For lengths of symbols
PUSH	For a subroutine to put symbols on a stack
POP	For a subroutine to remove symbols from a stack
STACK	For a stack of attributes
KEYVALUE	For an array of keyword values
DIGIT	For numeric characters
LETTER	For alphabetic characters
EOFMSG	For an end-of-file message

The rationale here is to develop a well-accepted set of naming conventions and to reduce the time spent by programmers in devising good mnemonic words. This standard is intended to promote program readability and to prevent confusion caused by having different names for the same entities.

[GEN-3]   *Each installation shall have established alignment (prettyprinting) conventions.*

The rationale here is also to promote readability and to save time by once and for all developing a fixed set of rules. The value of adopting rules for good program spacing is enormous. The tedium involved in alignment can be offset by an (automatic) formatting program. A specific set of alignment rules is given in Appendix B.

[GEN-4]   *No program unit may exceed two pages of code.*

The rationale here is to force program units (i.e., main programs, functions, or subroutines) to be isolated on at almost two pages of text. In general, each program unit should occupy no more than a single page of text. However, due to the frequent exceptional cases where initializations or repeated computations require extensive code, the standard allows program units to occupy up to two pages of text.

[GEN-5]   *All programs shall include the following comment:*

```
(*      **     PROGRAM TITLE              Brief title              *)
(*      **
(*      **     WRITTEN BY                 Name of author(s)        *)
(*      **     DATE WRITTEN               Date of first compilation *)
(*      **     WRITTEN FOR                Responsible unit         *)
(*      **
(*      **     PROGRAM SUMMARY            Brief program summary    *)
                     .
                     .
                     .

(*      **     INPUT AND OUTPUT FILES
(*      **         file-name:             Brief description of use *)
                     .
                     .
                     .
```

The rationale here is to give a quick synopsis of the program's intent, input and output files, and title information, so that a program has some minimal internal documentation.

DECLARATIONS

[DCL-1]   *All scalars that remain constant throughout a program must be specified in a constant declaration.*

The rationale here is to isolate constants and, if need be, to allow changes without affecting the logic in the executable statements. For example, use

```
CONST
    NUMOFELEMENTS   =   100;
    EPSILON         =   0.001;
    .
    .
    NUMOFHITS    :=   0;
    FOR INDEX    :=   1 TO NUMOFELEMENTS DO
```

```
        IF A [INDEX]  <  EPSILON  THEN
            NUMBEROFHITS  :=  NUMOFHITS  +  1;
            .
            .
            .
```

rather than

```
        NUMOFHITS  :=  0
        FOR INDEX  :=  1 TO 100 DO
            IF (A [INDEX]  <  0.001)  THEN
                NUMBEROFHITS  :=  NUMOFHITS  +  1;
                .
                .
                .
```

[DCL-2]   *Each program must have a (possibly empty) set of global
           variables selected by some designated person before any code is
           written. These are the only variables that can be used globally.*

The rationale here is to limit the number of global values and to discourage the often haphazard introduction of global variables as code is being developed.

[DLC-3]   *No function may alter any of its actual parameters or change the
           value of any global variable.*

The rationale here is to force a pure use of functions called within expressions, that is, to eliminate side effects within functions. For example,

```
FUNCTION OCCURS (SEARCHCHAR : CHARACTER;
                 CHARSTR     : STRING;
                 STRLENGTH   : INTEGER;
                 VAR ERROR   : BOOLEAN) : INTEGER;
    .
    .
    .

        IF (COUNT  >  STRLENGTH)  THEN
            BEGIN
                ERROR    :=  TRUE;
                OCCURS   :=  0
            END
        ELSE
```

```
BEGIN
      ERROR    :=    FALSE;
      OCCURS   :=    COUNT
END ;
```

```
END (*   OCCURS   *)
```

is not allowed. Instead, a procedure must be used.

[DLC-4]   *The parameters of a procedure must be declared with comments describing the logical role of each parameter.*

The rationale here is to give some minimal information on the logical role of the procedure. For example, use

```
PROCEDURE EXAMPLE  (* IN *)      A,B:       INTEGER;
                   (* INOUT *) VAR C,D:   INTEGER;
                   (* OUT *)    VAR E,F:   REAL);
```

The comments (* IN *), (* INOUT *), and (* OUT *) may be replaced by more informative comments, for example: (* USING *), (* UPDATING *), and (* GIVING *).

[DLC-5]   *The end of each procedure or function declaration must be followed by a comment giving the procedure or function name, e.g., END (*EXAMPLE*).*

CONTROL STRUCTURES

[CNTRL-1]   *GOTOs are not allowed.*

The rationale here is to force the programmers to *think ahead* and use only 1-in, 1-out control structures. Many programmers at first believe that this restriction is unreasonable. With some practice, programming with these control structures becomes quite easy. If it seems necessary to use a GOTO in another setting, the following alternatives should be considered:

1. Restructuring the algorithm
2. Putting blocks of code in a subroutine
3. Copying in a piece of code
4. Repeating a condition previously tested
5. Reversing a condition to its negative.

[CNTRL-2]   *Nesting of any combination of IF, FOR, WHILE, CASE, and REPEAT statements must be no more than four levels deep. An exception is allowed for simulating a generalized case statement.*

The rationale here is to prevent the human complexity that results from deeply nested control structures. An exception is allowed for IF statements that simulate a generalized case statement. For example,

IF   case __ 1   THEN

statement __ 1

ELSE IF   case __ 2   THEN

statement __ 2

.
.
.

ELSE IF   case __ n   THEN

statement __ n

counts as one level of nesting.

[CNTRL-3]   *The end of a case statement must be followed by the comment END (* CASE *).*

[CNTRL-4]   *Null statements must include a comment line, for example: (*DO NOTHING*).*

The rationale here is to make a null action explicit.

CONCLUSIONS

The general issue of program standards is indeed complex. When an attempt is made to restrict the initial boundaries of a language, the programmer resistance can be great. In addition, any attempt to promote or enforce such a set of program standards must resolve a number of difficult issues.

First, exceptional cases must be avoided when writing a standard. It is critical that the standard be as solid as possible, for otherwise, the credibility of the entire activity can be undermined. Possible exceptional cases must thus be carefully screened before the standard is adopted.

Second, there is the issue of enforcement. What mechanism should be set up to enforce the standards? Can the standards really be enforced without some kind of automatic aids? What about the professional programmer who does not see any reason for a particular standard or its use in a particular case? These questions are difficult to answer.

Third, given that some method of enforcement has been adopted and given that some useful exception does occur, how is the exception to be handled? While an ideal standard has no exceptions, when exceptions do arise, they have to be handled without undermining the credibility of the entire effort.

Fourth, there are a number of human factors that must be faced, especially when standards are being developed. For one, choices may be a matter of taste, and there are bound to be some arbitrary decisions. Further, there may be some initial overhead in following the standards. The human tendency is to get on with the job, i.e., code. This tendency must be resisted, for if the standards are correct, breaking the standards is shortsighted.

Finally, one must be very careful to avoid expecting too much from the standards, for eventually the problem-dependent features of a program will demand special attention. While the adoption of good standards may help in producing good solutions to the problem at hand, ultimately the style and expertise of the practicing programmer will become paramount.

"Progress is our most important product."
Advertising slogan of General Electric Corporation

SELECTING MNEMONIC NAMES

When writing PASCAL programs, it is very tempting to use short and often uninformative user-defined names. The temptation arises because of the extra effort required to devise and actually code more illuminating (usually longer) names. Nevertheless, the choice of user-defined names has a psychological impact that cannot be ignored. Consider the two simple program fragments in Example 5.1. Of the two, Example 5.1b is the more lucid procedure for reading a sequence of numeric values and printing the maximum.

Good mnemonic names are a powerful tool for clear documentation, easy verification, and ready maintenance. We offer four basic principles for devising user-defined names:

1. Use standard names and standard abbreviations as much as possible.
2. Choose names that activate the correct "psychological set" [Ref. W1].
3. Avoid names that are not "psychologically distant" [Ref. W1].
4. Be sure to follow consistent naming conventions and avoid names that can be confused with a system name or a PASCAL keyword.

Standard Names and Abbreviations

We encourage the adoption of a full set of standard names and abbreviations for every major programming application. For programmers working on a team or modifying someone else's code, the value of standard mnemonics is

Example 5.1 Using Good Mnemonic Names

5.1a Poor

```
VAR
   N, INDEX: INTEGER;
   X, BIG  : REAL;

BEGIN

   READLN(N, X);

   BIG := X;

   FOR INDEX := 1 TO N DO
      BEGIN

         READLN(X);

         IF BIG < X THEN
            BIG := X

      END;

   WRITELN('THE LARGEST VALUE = ', BIG)

END
```

5.1b Better

```
VAR
   NUMOFVALUES, INDEX: INTEGER;
   NEWVALUE, MAXVALUE: REAL;


BEGIN

   READLN(NUMOFVALUES, NEWVALUE);

   MAXVALUE := NEWVALUE;

   FOR INDEX := 1 TO NUMOFVALUES DO
      BEGIN

         READLN(NEWVALUE);

         IF MAXVALUE < NEWVALUE THEN
            MAXVALUE := NEWVALUE

      END;

   WRITELN('THE LARGEST VALUE = ', MAXVALUE)

END
```

---

obvious. Even if you are a student, your instructor may wish to choose standard names for an assignment to simplify understanding of everyone's program.

A formal set of standard names and abbreviations makes the selection of names easy. If your instructor, customer, or programming manager wants an input record to have the name, MASTER, or a value on a graph to have the name, YCOORD, then these are the "best" names to use, for they make a program consistent with established conventions.

If you have no formal set of standard names or abbreviations, informal standard names and abbreviations are often available. In the case of a grading program, names like SCORE, GRADE, or MEAN are illuminating informal standards. Furthermore, PASCAL programmers have their own familiar conventions, for example:

SUM	For summing elements in an array
IDNUM	For identification numbers
DENOM	For denominators of fractions
AVERAGE	For averages
ERROR	For error flags
TOTALERROR	For total accumulated error values
EPSILON	For error tolerances

The use of words such as these makes a program consistent with informal conventions.

As for standard abbreviations, a good place to start is a dictionary. The PASCAL limitation to names without a break character makes abbreviations sometimes confusing. Despite this awkward inconvenience, you must make sure that abbreviations are well understood. What better place to start than your dictionary?

Psychological Set

In psychology, the term "psychological set" means a readiness to respond in a specific way to certain stimuli. In the programming context, a "psychological set" means a readiness to associate particular entities or properties with a word. Entities such as social security numbers, rates of pay, and people's names have many possible word representations. It is important that the psychological set activated by a particular name be "correct" (i.e., represent the intended entity). Of course, the psychological set activated by a particular name differs for different people.

Creating a name with the correct psychological set can be difficult. Often it is easy to pick a name with a close but dangerously incorrect psychological set. As an example, suppose a programmer decided to represent a file of sale transaction cards, and the record's three fields (the identification of the salesperson, the identification of the item sold, and the quantity of the item sold) with the respective names INPUT, FIELD1, FIELD2, and FIELD3. The name INPUT might cause a reader to associate an arbitrary deck of cards with the input data. A better choice would be SALEFILE. Likewise, the data names FIELD1, FIELD2, and FIELD3 are less clear than PERSONID, ITEMID, and QUANTITY SOLD.

Another aspect of psychological set arises when names have no specific semantic role. For example, a programmer may define an array whose subscripts do not correspond to any meaningful object in the real world, or he may define a function of purely mathematical arguments. In both cases, a standard name should be used. For example, subscripts are generally denoted by I, J, or K; functions by F, G, or H; and arguments by X, Y, or Z. Often these familiar conventions will lend understanding. For example,

$$I = F(X,Y)$$

is more suggestive than

$$Y = X(I,F)$$

if the left-hand side denotes an integer-valued variable and the right-hand side denotes the application of a function to two arbitrary real variables.

A name that is an abbreviation for a longer conceptual unit can also be hazardous, especially when the resulting abbreviation is an acronym that activates a psychological set for another entity. For example, a programmer who desires a name for a rate of pay entry would be unwise to use the name ROPE, which does not semantically reflect the entity's true value. The temptation, of course, is to think of a heavy cord of intertwined fibers.

Words like FIELD1, FIELD2, and FIELD3 should be avoided for still another reason. Suppose that the format of a transaction card was changed so that the sales person identification number became the third field instead of the first field, and the item sold number became the first instead of the second field, etc. The word FIELD1 must then be changed to FIELD3, FIELD2 to FIELD1, etc. Needless to say, it is highly possible that some occurrence of the word FIELD3 might not be changed to FIELD1! Finding a mistake like the printer just made in the last sentence is another problem with such words.

Another important aspect of psychological set is the effect of abbreviations. The first point to remember is that you should only abbreviate after you have created a full mnemonic name. Second, the chosen abbreviation should not activate a psychological set different from the original name. Let us assume you have created the lengthy mnemonic name OWNER-IDENTIFICATION-NUMBER and that it activates the correct psychological set. Even though you must abbreviate the name, you should reject such abbreviations as ONO or OWNID, for they may very well be misleading. A word like IDNUM is preferable. Admittedly, a good solution to the problem is hard to devise.

Psychological Distance

In addition to finding a proper name for each entity, you should choose names for different entities that are "psychologically distant" enough to avoid confusion. Since the distance concept is related to the psychology of the programmer, it resists formalization. Loosely speaking, names that look alike, sound alike, are spelled alike, or have similar meanings are not psychologically distant.

Consider the following pairs of names along with the indication of their distance:

	Name for One Entity	Name for Another Entity	Distance
(a)	BKRPNT	BRKPNT	Almost invisible
(b)	MOVRF	MOVLF	Almost none
(c)	CODE	KODE	Small
(d)	IDEN	IDENT	Small
(e)	OMEGA	DELTA	Large
(f)	ROOT	DISCRIMINANT	Large and informative

In this table the distance between pairs of names is small, except for entries (e) and (f). As for (a) through (d), good luck! Entry (a) shows two discrete names, but in a program could you be sure that one is not a typing or key punching error? In general, shy away from using "close" names.

Consider entry (b), which is taken from an actual program. The names had the following meanings:

Name (Argument)	Meaning
MOVLF(SQ1)	MOVE *left from* square SQ1
MOVLT(SQ1)	MOVE *left to* square SQ1
MOVRF(SQ1)	MOVE *right from* square SQ1
MOVRT(SQ1)	MOVE *right to* square SQ1

The programmer in this case wrote four functions, subprograms, that required a square on a checkerboard as an argument. The input square was denoted by SQ1, and the value returned by the function was TRUE or FALSE, depending on whether it was possible to move left or right, from or to, the square SQ1 given as input. The choice of names, good on initial consideration, resulted in a series of errors. The programmer unfortunately confused MOVLF and MOVRF. It *literally* took days to discover this mistake.

Other Considerations

A programmer should also be sure that all user-defined names exhibit "uniformity." This is also a difficult notion to formalize. In rough terms, all user-defined names that imply similar properties should be of similar form. For example, consider the previous maximum value example. It would be unfortunate to choose the names

> NUM
> NEXT
> BIGVAL

even though they can activate the correct psychological set and are psychologically distant, for this pair of data names does not follow a uniform coding scheme. A better choice of names is

> NUMOFVALUES
> NEXTVALUE
> MAXVALUE

The programmer is especially advised to keep abbreviations uniform.

Before using a name in a program, the programmer should also make sure that it is not a system name or a PASCAL keyword. It is handy to keep a list of keywords and a list of system names.

GLOBAL VARIABLES, FUNCTIONS, AND PROCEDURES

Global Variables

The use of variables to represent updated entities is familiar to all programmers. Guidelines for the effective use of variables are seldom discussed. Nevertheless, this topic is of paramount importance in writing quality programs.

Consider a "block" (i.e., a sequence of statements) of code, B, that performs some computation, f, on two variables, X1 and X2, to yield a result, Y, as illustrated in Fig. 5.1. In any such block there may, of course, be other

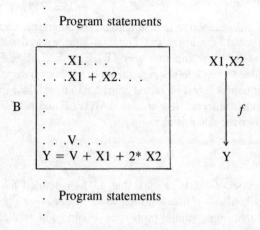

Fig. 5.1 A "block" of code

intermediate variables needed for the computation. Assume for the moment that each of the intermediate variables is not used outside the block of code B except for one variable, V. In order to abstract the computation f in B, one must then not only consider the computation of Y from X1 and X2, but also consider the effect on V. In this case we say that V is "active in" or "global to" the block.

The use of multiple global variables is a frequent cause of undue complexity in computer programs. To abstract the computation of a logical block of code, the changes applied to global variables must be considered.

There are several critical problems associated with the use of multiple global variables. First, the complexity of a block of statements rapidly increases with even a small increase in the number of variables. Second, if the number of statements over which the variables range is large, then the intent of referencing statements can be difficult to comprehend. Importantly, any change to a program outside the block of statements can affect the correctness of the block itself.

The concept of global variables in PASCAL is most evident in the case of variables that are external to a function or procedure. The examples which follow take advantage of this circumstance. But the concept should be understood in terms of *any* block of code that has the *effect* of a function or procedure.

Example 5.2 Functions and Procedures

5.2a A Simple Function

```
FUNCTION AREA(RADIUS: REAL): REAL;

CONST
   PI = 3.14159;

BEGIN

   AREA := PI * (RADIUS*RADIUS)

END;
```

5.2b A Simple Procedure

```
PROCEDURE GETAREA(RADIUS: REAL; VAR AREA: REAL);

CONST
   PI = 3.14159;

BEGIN

   AREA := PI * (RADIUS*RADIUS)

END;
```

PASCAL is careful to make the following (commonly held) distinction. A "function" refers to a subprogram that returns a value. A "procedure " refers to a subprogram that produces a change in a variable outside the subprogram. In particular, consider the simple declarations of Example 5.2. In Example 5.2a, the subprogram AREA is used as a function. For example, if the value of R is 3.0, an evaluation of the expression

$$1.0 + AREA(R)$$

yields one, plus the value of the function. In Example 5.2b the subprogram AREA is used as a procedure. For example, if the value of RADIUS is 3.0, the statement

$$GETAREA(R, AREA)$$

results in assigning to AREA the value computed by the procedure. The difference between functions and procedures is important but not always obvious. Generally speaking, functions are used in place of *expressions* to return *values*, whereas procedures are used in place of *statements* to perform *assignments* to variables. It is possible in PASCAL to write subprograms that both return a value and cause an effect outside the subprogram. As a rule, it is unwise to do this, as we shall see in subsequent examples.

Functions

Loosely speaking, the *context* of a function is its relation to other sections of a program. If a function alters a quantity global to itself, then it exhibits a *context effect*. Basically, a function can produce a context effect in two ways: by altering its arguments or by altering a global variable.

Programmers who write functions with context effects can get unpleasant surprises. Consider Example 5.3. These two program segments are identical except for the replacement of the expression

$$F(B) + F(B)$$

in Example 5.3a by the expression

$$2.0*F(B)$$

in Example 5.3b. These two programs are not equivalent because

$$F(B) + F(B) = (11.0)*(3.0) + (12.0)*(3.0)$$
$$= 69.0$$
$$2.0*F(B) = (2.0)*(11.0)*(3.0)$$
$$= 66.0$$

Hence we lose a fundamental property of addition. The problem is caused by the context effect in the function F with the assignment of (A + 1.0) to A, where A is global to the function.

Example 5.3 Context Effect Accompanying the Returned Value of a Function

5.3a One Program

```
VAR
    A, B, C: REAL;


FUNCTION F(X: REAL): REAL;

BEGIN

    A := A + 1;
    F := A * X

END;


BEGIN

    A := 10;
    B := 3;
    C := F(B) + F(B);

    WRITELN(C)

END
```

5.3b An Equivalent Program?

```
VAR
    A, B, C: REAL;


FUNCTION F(X: REAL): REAL;

BEGIN

    A := A + 1;
    F := A * X

END;

BEGIN

    A := 10;
    B := 3;
    C := 2 * F(B);

    WRITELN(C)

END
```

A similar case arises in Example 5.4. Again these examples are identical except that

$$F(B) + G(B)$$

in 5.4a is replaced by

$$G(B) + F(B)$$

in 5.4b. Using a left-to-right evaluation, the written values for C, 72 and 75, are not the same. Here, the familiar commutative property of addition is lost because of the assignment to a global variable. Certainly many programmers would be surprised to learn that $F(B) + G(B)$ is not equivalent in this case to $G(B) + F(B)$. Since PASCAL employs conventional mathematical notation, it is danger-

Example 5.4   Context Effect Accompanying an Assignment to a Global Variable

---

5.4a   One Program

```
VAR
    A, B, C: REAL;


FUNCTION F(X: REAL): REAL;

BEGIN

    A := A + 1;
    F := A * X

END;


FUNCTION G(X: REAL): REAL;

BEGIN

    A := A + 2;
    G := A * X

END;


BEGIN

    A := 10;
    B := 3;
    C := F(B) + G(B);

    WRITELN(C)

END
```

5.4b An Equivalent Program?

```
VAR
   A, B, C: REAL;


FUNCTION F(X: REAL): REAL;

BEGIN

   A := A + 1;
   F := A * X

END;


FUNCTION G(X: REAL): REAL;
BEGIN

   A := A + 2;
   G := A * X

END;

BEGIN

   A := 10;
   B := 3;
   C := G(B) + F(B);

   WRITELN(C)

END
```

---

ous to write functions that violate the properties of established mathematical systems.

The case against context effects becomes even more severe when we need to change a program. Change is a daily occurrence in programming. Someone may find a more efficient algorithm, more output may be needed, a bug may be detected, or revised specifications may be given. If a piece of code to be changed has context effects, then those effects must be accounted for. The resulting changes may imply the need to delve deeply into the entire program for a clear understanding of what effects a function or procedure has on other parts of the program. Adding a few extra lines of code for that desirable change may kill the correctness of another piece of code. As a result, another change may be needed to right matters, and so on. Even if this process succeeds, it is not likely to add to the clarity or flexibility of the program. Had the original program been written without context effects, the function could be changed *without* looking at the rest of the program.

Next consider Example 5.5, a case in which a function subprogram alters the value of an argument. The problem here is that two function calls with the same arguments return *different* values. In larger programs, such a use of arguments is quite dangerous. In making a correction or alteration, the programmer may unwittingly alter the value of subsequent calls to the function. Furthermore, to replace F with another procedure, the programmer must consider the main program in order to ensure the proper handling of global variables.

In short, functions with context effects are to be avoided, unless there is a compelling reason to use them.

Procedures

The purpose of a procedure is to produce some effect external to itself, not to return a value. Essentially, a procedure consists of a group of statements isolated from a main routine or program for convenience or clarity. The problems encountered with context effects in procedures are quite similar to those encountered in functions. There is one important exception. Since a procedure is designed to update a specific set of variables, each of the changed variables should be included in the list of arguments. Consider Example 5.6. By using all assigned variables in the argument list in each procedure call, the reader can speed up tracing the changed variables, since he will not have to look through the body of the procedure.

Example 5.5 Context Effect on the Arguments of a Function

```
VAR
    A, B, C: REAL;


FUNCTION F(X: REAL; VAR Y: REAL): REAL;

BEGIN

    Y := Y + X;
    F := X * Y

END;


BEGIN

    A := 4;
    B := F(5, A);
    C := F(5, A);

    WRITELN(B, C)

END
```

Example 5.6 Context Effect in Procedures by Assignment to a Global Variable

---

5.6a Poor

```
VAR
    A, B: REAL;


PROCEDURE P(VAR X: REAL);

BEGIN

    X := 2 * (X + 1);
    B := 5 * X

END;


BEGIN

    A := 17;
    B :=  3;
    P(A);

    WRITELN(A, B)

END
```

5.6b Better

```
VAR
    A, B: REAL;

PROCEDURE P(VAR X, Y: REAL);

BEGIN

    X := 2 * (X + 1);
    Y := 5 * X

END;

BEGIN

    A := 17;
    B :=  3;
    P(A, B);

    WRITELN(A, B)

END
```

Exceptions to the Rules and Summary

There are, of course, cases where global variables and context effects may indeed be useful. For example, there may be names and arrays whose (often used) values remain constant within the program. Making these quantities global to the entire program certainly causes no problems. The global use of the legal move mappings in the Kriegspiel program illustrates this point.

More importantly, there may be variables and arrays whose values do change but are used in so many procedures that passing them as arguments in every call would result in a lengthy or inefficient code. The global use of the BOARD array to represent the current board status in the Kriegspiel program illustrates this point. In such cases, it may be justifiable to make the quantities global to all procedures.

Nevertheless, global variables and context effects can cause serious problems. If they are used, they should be used sparingly. In summary, we give the following rules of thumb:

1. *Functions*
   Use a function only for its returned value.
   Do not use a function when you need a subroutine.
   Do not alter formal parameters.
   Do not alter global variables.

2. *Procedures*
   Do not use a procedure when you need a function.
   Do not alter global variables.

3. *Both*
   Be very careful when you use global variables.

RECURSION

Loosely speaking, recursion is a method of definition in which the object being defined is used within the definition. For example, consider the following definition of the word "descendant":

A descendant of a person is a son or daughter of the person, or a descendant of a son or daughter.

In this definition *all* the descendants of the person are simply and precisely accounted for. A nonrecursive definition of "descendant" that takes all possibilities into consideration would be the following:

A descendant of a person is a son or daughter of the person, or a grandson or granddaughter of the person, or a great-grandson or great-granddaughter of the person, etc.

In this case, the definition is lengthier and less succinct than the recursive definition. It is interesting to note how dictionaries attempt to skirt recursion in the definition of "descendant." "Descendant" is often defined in terms of "ancestor," whereas "ancestor" is defined in terms of "descendant." The two definitions are, in fact, mutually recursive.

In programming, recursive definitions apply to function and procedure declarations. A recursive subprogram declaration is one that has the potential to invoke itself. In other words, it is defined partially in terms of itself.

The primary point of this section is that in many instances recursive definitions are clearer, more succinct, or more natural, than their nonrecursive counterparts, even if they are less efficient. Recursive definitions often follow naturally using the top-down programming approach. A clear idea of the nature and power of recursive definitions can be a valuable aid to a PASCAL programmer.

Suppose we wish to sum the elements of an integer array. Simple arithmetic gives us the following equality:

$$\sum_{i=1}^{n} a_i = a_1 \qquad \text{if } n = 1$$

$$\sum_{i=1}^{n} a_i = a_n + \sum_{i=1}^{n-1} a_i \qquad \text{if } n \geqslant 2$$

Stated in English, the sum of the elements of an array is the last element plus the sum of the first $n - 1$ elements. If the array has only one element, the sum is the single element. With these facts in mind, it is possible to write the function SUM recursively, as in Example 5.7a. Its nonrecursive counterpart is given in Example 5.7b.

To ensure that the recursive definition of SUM is understood, observe the following analysis of the function subprogram when applied to a four-element array containing the numbers 3, 6, 8, and 2.

Depth of Recursive Calls	Value of SUM
1	SUM(A,4)
2	2 + SUM(A,3)
3	2 + (8 + SUM(A,2))
4	2 + (8 + (6 + SUM(A,1)))
4	2 + (8 + (6 + 3))
3	2 + (8 + 9)
2	2 + 17
1	19

Example 5.7 Sum of the Elements in an Array Defined with and without Recursion

---

5.7a   Recursive Definition

```
TYPE
  ANARRAY = ARRAY[1..10] OF INTEGER;


FUNCTION SUM(A: ANARRAY;  N: INTEGER): INTEGER;

BEGIN

    IF N = 1
       THEN
          SUM := A[1]
       ELSE
          SUM := A[N] + SUM(A, N-1)

END;
```

5.7b   Nonrecursive Definition

```
TYPE
   ANARRAY = ARRAY[1..10] OF INTEGER;

FUNCTION SUM(A: ANARRAY;  N: INTEGER): INTEGER;

VAR
   INDEX: INTEGER;

BEGIN

   SUM := 0;

   FOR INDEX := 1 TO N DO
      SUM := SUM + A[INDEX]

END;
```

An example particularly well suited to recursive definition is the implementation of Euclid's algorithm for computing the greatest common divisor of two positive integers, M and N. The GCD function subprogram requires an additional integer function MOD(I,J) that returns the remainder when I is divided by J.

The definitions are shown in Example 5.8. For comparison, a nonrecursive definition for the same function subprogram is also given. The nonrecursive definitions are slightly larger and less clear. The properties of the algorithm are still present, but they are hidden by the looping constructs.

Merely knowing what recursion looks like is not enough. It is also necessary to know (1) if recursion is applicable to the problem at hand, and (2) how to apply it. There are no formal rules in either case, but are some guidelines. One is that the notion of mathematical "induction" is a close analog to recursion. Induction is a method of definition in which (1) initial values of a function are defined explicitly (the base step), and (2) other values are implicitly defined in terms of previous values (the inductive step). If the definition given in the second step applies to all elements other than the initial values, then the principle of mathematical induction asserts that the function is (explicitly) well-defined for all values in its domain.

To illustrate the method of inductive definition, consider the sequence of Fibonacci numbers. The first two numbers are both 1, and each successive number in the sequence is the sum of the two preceding numbers. More explicitly,

$$N = 1 \quad \text{BASE STEP} \qquad F(1) = 1$$
$$N = 2 \qquad\qquad\qquad\quad F(2) = 1$$

$$N \geq 3 \quad \text{INDUCTIVE STEP} \qquad F(N) = F(N-1) + F(N-2)$$

Example 5.8 Euclid's Greatest Common Divisor Algorithm Defined with and without Recursion

5.8a   Recursive Definition

```
FUNCTION GCD(FIRSTNUM, SECONDNUM: INTEGER): INTEGER;

VAR
   REMAINDER: INTEGER;

BEGIN

   IF FIRSTNUM < SECONDNUM
      THEN
         GCD := GCD(SECONDNUM, FIRSTNUM)

      ELSE
         BEGIN

            REMAINDER := FIRSTNUM MOD SECONDNUM;

            IF REMAINDER = 0
               THEN
                  GCD := SECONDNUM
               ELSE
                  GCD := GCD(SECONDNUM, REMAINDER)

         END

END;
```

5.8b Nonrecursive Definition

```
FUNCTION GCD(FIRSTNUM, SECONDNUM: INTEGER): INTEGER;

VAR
    REMAINDER, LOVALUE, HIVALUE: INTEGER;

BEGIN

    HIVALUE := MAX(FIRSTNUM, SECONDNUM);
    LOVALUE := MIN(FIRSTNUM, SECONDNUM);

    REMAINDER := HIVALUE MOD LOVALUE;

    IF REMAINDER = 0
        THEN
            GCD := LOVALUE

        ELSE
            BEGIN

                REPEAT

                    REMAINDER := HIVALUE MOD LOVALUE;
                    HIVALUE   := LOVALUE;
                    LOVALUE   := REMAINDER

                UNTIL (REMAINDER = 0);

                GCD := HIVALUE

            END

END;
```

The step from this inductive definition to a recursive function declaration is small. A function subprogram to generate the Nth Fibonacci number is shown defined recursively and nonrecursively in Example 5.9. The Fibonacci function written recursively parrots the inductive definition and clearly shows the main property of the Fibonacci numbers. While the nonrecursive example uses the same property, it is harder to detect. The additional code required to write the function nonrecursively is mostly bookkeeping. Also note that in the recursive definition, the function subprogram FIB is recursively invoked twice. Without a good optimizing compiler, this double invocation is quite inefficient.

A great deal could be said about recursion, and a good deal of the literature is devoted to the subject. For our purposes, the point is simple. Understand the use of recursion and the translation from a recursive definition to a nonrecursive PASCAL code. You may find that recursion is a valuable addition to your programming skills.

Example 5.9 The Fibbonacci Sequence Defined with and without Recursion

---

5.9a Recursive Definition

```
FUNCTION FIB(N: INTEGER): INTEGER;

BEGIN

   IF N <= 2
      THEN
         FIB := 1
      ELSE
         FIB := FIB(N-1) + FIB(N-2)

END;
```

5.9b Nonrecursive Definition

```
FUNCTION FIB(N: INTEGER): INTEGER;

VAR
   F1, F2, INDEX: INTEGER;

BEGIN

   IF N <= 2
      THEN
         FIB := 1
      ELSE
         BEGIN

            F1 := 1;
            F2 := 1;

            FOR INDEX := 3 TO N DO
               BEGIN
                  FIB := F1 + F2;
                  F1  := F2;
                  F2  := FIB
               END

         END

END;
```

THE OVERCONCERN WITH MICROEFFICIENCY

Machine efficiency has been one of the most frequent concerns of managers, instructors, and programmers alike. In the early years of computing, when hardware configurations were small and slow, it was important to use as little storage space or computer time as possible. Since then, digital computers have become large, inexpensive, and fast. In addition, virtual memory has been incorporated into many systems. Yet there is still frequent concern with the question of machine efficiency because of the need to control programming costs.

The reasons for striving for machine efficiency are not only historic and economic; there is also a certain human element. Programmers take pride in their ability to squeeze out excess lines of code or to use an appropriate efficiency feature, and managers take a natural pride in the speed of their programs or their compact use of storage.

The Real Costs

While we do not at all question the need to reduce programming costs, we do believe that this concern is often focused on the wrong issues. For example, some typical concerns in PASCAL programming are the following:

1. Using numerous global variables.
2. Avoiding procedures and functions.
3. Making use of GOTOs.
4. Writing IF statements so that the most frequent conditions are checked first.

These rules are intended to save space and execution time, thus lowering costs. Because of the often rather small and local savings afforded by the above techniques, we shall call the efficiency they provide "microefficiency" [Ref. A1]. With the development of inexpensive fast storage and virtual memory systems, the preoccupation with the size and speed of machine code would seem to have been dealt a death blow. Not so! Old habits remain.

The concern with microefficiency has often obscured the really important programming costs. The first issue is to understand the problem completely and make sure that the resulting specification satisfies the user. The second issue is to produce high-quality system design, clear code, and clear documentation. The final issue, and only if necessary, is to produce a fast or compact program.

While microefficient programs do help to reduce overall costs, in the larger perspective, they are usually only a small factor. The total cost of a system includes the costs of promotion, time needed to understand user requirements, the development of clear and acceptable specifications, program writing, documentation, and above all, maintenance. If a proposed programming system is not acceptable to the ultimate user, further development is wasted. If specifications are not adequate, system development is often misdirected and delayed. If there is a failure to recognize exceptional conditions and different solution strategies or if there is a poor initial design, the success of any development effort is undermined. Moreover, program development costs include programmer training, thinking time, coding time, and the time and effort needed to integrate a subsystem into an overall system. Documentation costs include the time needed to prepare reports, figures, and summaries of existing code.

In the life of many large programs, the largest cost factor is system maintenance. Maintenance of an ill-conceived, poorly developed, poorly coded, or poorly documented system is expensive and time consuming at best. More typically, program performance is seriously degraded. Easy maintenance of itself can yield greater savings than microefficient program performance. To control programming costs, we must look in the right places.

Program Performance

There are, of course, cases where the costs of program performance are significant. Perhaps a given program will be run every day, a given data file may be accessed every hour, or fast memory may be scarce. In these cases, attention should be devoted to the *top* levels of program design where "macroefficient" techniques can be applied.

It does little good to scatter time and space microefficiencies all over the code if the file and array organizations are not optimal. At an even higher level, file and array techniques will be of little avail if the entire program frequently needs to be restarted because of the errors due to the improper input of data. In such cases, perhaps several sequentially executed programs with local and less severe restraints should be designed and substituted for one large program. At the highest level, if the whole program is more easily handled without a digital computer, all the concern with computer performance cost is meaningless.

A rather significant issue stems from the following observation. It is estimated that 90 percent of the CPU time in a program is spent on 10 percent of the code. If a programmer is faced with program performance demands, the first consideration should be *where* the program is losing its time. Microefficiency can then be spent on this 10 percent of the code.

Finally, if a program is designing low-level portions of code and really needs microefficient techniques, caution is still in order. Considerations such as parking characters in integer values or avoiding character types can make a program quite machine dependent. Tight, tricky, microefficient code can be almost impossible for another person to understand. These performance savings may in the end raise the cost of program maintenance.

The overriding points of our discussion can be summarized as follows. The concern with program microefficiency is often shortsighted. The primary concern should be to consider overall program costs and to place major economic emphasis on earlier phases of program development. There is a lot of money being wasted in the production of poor definitions, poor designs, poor documentation, and in the development of slipshod programs.

THE CASE AGAINST PROGRAM FLOWCHARTS

In 1947, H. H. Goldstine and J. von Neumann [Ref. G1] introduced a pictorial notation called a "flow diagram." Its purpose was to facilitate the translation of algorithms into machine language programs. The flow diagrams pictured the course of machine control through a sequence of steps and indicated the contents and change of items in storage. Since then these ideas and notations, along with various diagrams and charts used in business system analysis [Ref. C4], have been absorbed into almost all areas of electronic data processing. The basic concept has come to be known as "flowcharting." We can roughly distinguish between two types of flowcharts: system flowcharts and program flowcharts.

System flowcharts describe the flow of major data items and the control sequence of major operations in an information-processing system. It is customary to picture the relationship existing between information, media, equipment, equipment operations, and manual operations. An example is given in Fig. 5.2. There are few specific details, and only a rough picture of the overall process. As with document flowcharts, system flowcharts concentrate more on the flow of data than on the flow of control.

Program flowcharts specify details of the sequential flow of control through an actual program. A familiar example is Fig. 5.3. Program flowcharts

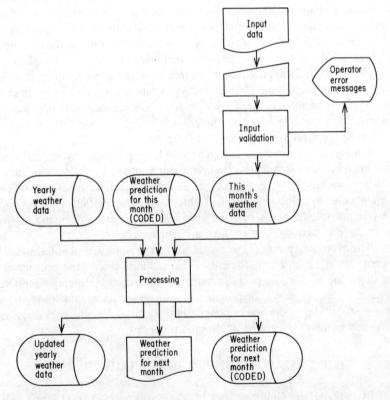

Fig. 5.2   A system flowchart for end-of-month weather analysis

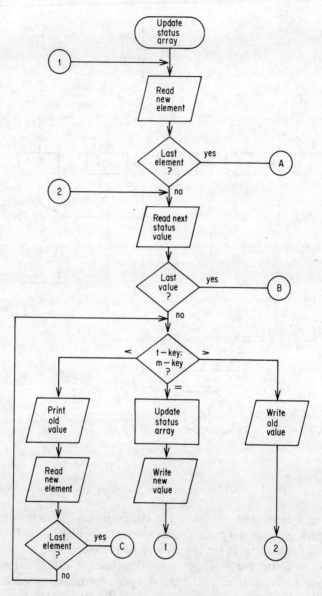

Fig. 5.3 A strange program

are the most direct descendant of Goldstine and von Neumann's flow diagrams, for both describe the flow of control in great detail. It is interesting to note that program flowcharts do not explicitly describe the data flow, as was the case with the original flow diagrams.

As for system flowcharts, we believe that they can be useful aids in

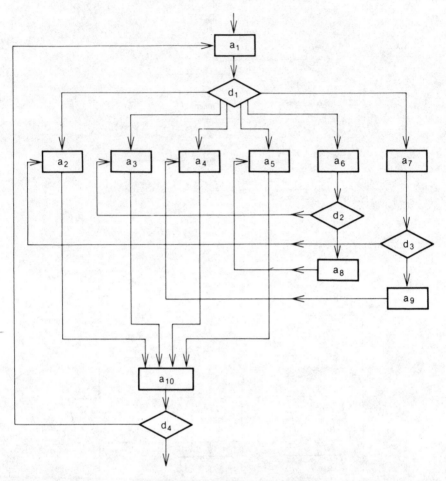

Fig. 5.4   A program flowchart schema

describing systems and processes. For documentation, system flowcharts can give a quick synopsis of a process. Unfortunately, the use of these flowcharts has sometimes been mistaken for complete problem description.

Our concern here is with program flowcharts, a technique familiar to all programmers and one often used daily. It is perhaps true that program flowcharts can assist in the design of very efficient, small algorithms. However, we believe that program flowcharts can easily suppress much useful information in favor of highlighting sequential control flow, something which distracts the programmer from the important functional relationship in the overall design. This in turn may obscure the use of alternative designs via the use of procedures and subprograms, the use of more intuitive data structures, or even the simple fine tuning of logic.

Consider the program flowchart schema in Fig. 5.4. The a_i stand for certain actions (e.g., assignments or procedure calls); the d_i stand for decisions. The programmer who derived this flowchart was so concerned with lines and boxes (i.e., sequences of steps) that the resulting code, while correct, tended to obscure the overall functional logic.

Other design methods resulted in a different solution, which was not as brief as that obtained from program flowcharts, but easier to understand. Figure 5.5 pictures the control flow derived from this new code.

One important problem with program flowcharts is keeping track of variables that change from one part of the flowchart to the next. A user who is preoccupied with flow of control details may quickly be in the position of the tourist to Boston who decides to drive his own car to see the sights. By not taking a sight-seeing bus, the visitor quickly gets distracted in the confusion of alternative routes.

Thinking back, were you ever asked to update or correct a program in which the documentation included program flowcharts? How often did you utilize them? Our observations indicate little such use of the charts. In the majority of cases the use of program flowcharts is replaced by a careful study of

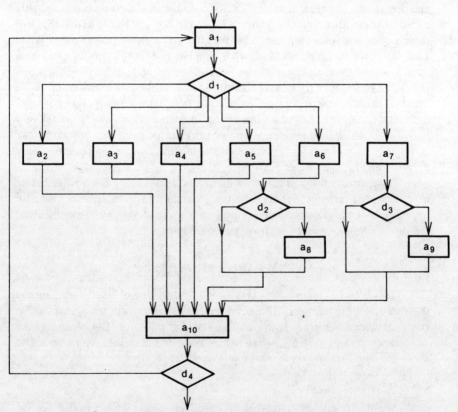

Fig. 5.5   Program flowchart schema derived from alternative code

the code that produced them in the first place. Good code alone seems to be sufficient for the detailed understanding needed for program maintenance.

Program flowcharts have less severe deficiencies. One is a general untidiness caused by the simple human limitation in the art of drawing straight lines and figures, which makes flowcharting a time-consuming activity as well. Also, who in tarnation borrowed my template?

Besides its somewhat awkward notation, did you ever notice that a program flowchart always seems to spill over the margin of the paper used to draw it on? Look back at Figure 5.3. This flowchart requires numerous connectors and page skipping to read the result. After reading a few pages, who knows where you came from, never mind where you are going. Even if you manage to keep connectors to a minimum to prevent mental page flipping, data processing still involves many conditional checks (i.e., branches) in flowcharts. When you connect all these branches to their logical destinations, you may see what is known as the "spaghetti effect," which is a profusion of crisscrossing branches.

Because of the rather large amount of time and work required to construct program flowcharts, program designers are naturally reluctant to rethink things and perhaps make a change or two. Even if a design modification is conceptually simple, the modification may require a flowchart box and line insertion that will force a complete redrawing just to get the chart to fit nicely on one page. When used for program documentation, what happens to flowcharts after a program modification? Even if someone else is assigned to update the program flowcharts, he or she may try to save time by squeezing the modifications in on the existing charts, perhaps in a different color ink. After a few years and many modifications one may have an interesting, modernistic work of art but a very poor flowchart. If a flowchart generator program is available, this effect can admittedly be avoided; however, the results of flowchart generators are usually no more helpful than the original code.

In summary, programmers and managers should really think twice before using time and resources for constructing program flowcharts, whether it be for program design or documentation. For good program design we recommend the top-down approach, which is discussed in Chapter 3.

VERY LARGE PROGRAMS

This book has focused on a single topic: the writing of quality programs by the individual programmer. The development of large software systems obviously involves other issues far beyond the scope of this book. But because of the importance of large systems, we introduce some of the quality issues here. Our ideas are based mainly on the work of Cave [Ref. C1].

Premises

We begin with a number of premises that we believe are vital for the success of any large programming project.

1. *The development of user-oriented software systems is first and foremost a management problem.*

This is a difficult premise to accept because poor management reflects right to the top of any organization. Nevertheless, this premise is vital since project failures are generally the result of improper or inexperienced management and not a lack of technical ability. The management responsibility requires not only knowledge, experience, and judgment, but also a high level of perspective. To avoid major mistakes in policy, it is vital to have a good perspective of

   a. The experience, skills, and tools required to complete a given task
   b. The availability of these resources within the organization
   c. The importance of establishing the credibility of outside experts through reliable references
   d. The need for constant vigilance against the dangers of sacrificing effectiveness for program efficiency.

2. *The success of any software system is always finally measured by the ultimate user.*

In order for capable managers to succeed, they must have an environment that responds quickly and is easily controlled. The willingness on the part of prospective users to order and pay for services rendered on a continuing basis is the essential element for effective control. When "dollar control" flows directly from the end user down through the ranks of the developer, it creates an environment less prone to politics, cleverness, and internal disagreements.

Measuring management ability largely by user satisfaction also creates a willingness on the part of management to call on outside expertise and forces attention on the need for accurate performance measurement.

This environment concept closely relates to Baker's work [Ref. B1]. The chief programmer team is organized around a chief with exceptional experience and control. One gets the feeling that this chief has one finger on the pulse of the entire project, while the tips of the other fingers control all members of the team. Within certain organizations, only a strong technical ability backed by strong personal credibility can create the environment needed to provide control and to obtain response from a team of programmers. The chief programmer team approach thus appears suitable for creating the management control essential to success in most organizations.

3. *The overall project management must not be divorced from software development.*

Independent of the individual system characteristics, and a highly technical environment notwithstanding, overall project management must be directly responsible for developing the software.

First, it is all too easy to blame software failures on any organizational unit other than the one under question. Identifying the project management with the technical problems ensures that management is indeed responsible for the entire effort.

Second, over and above the development of programs, the very nature of software development implies the need to develop the organization and managing procedures to be used in final operational systems. This decision-making process is implicitly given to the software developer. The reason, which is not readily apparent, is that the very nature of software development implicitly places the responsibility for designing a usable system upon those doing the creating, and not upon the user.

4. Software development must be a sequence of clearly isolated phases.

Changes *will* occur in project emphasis, personnel, time frames, user requirements, and the development environment. This implies that it is necessary to:

a. Allow time for the developer to gain experience and to discover the peculiarities of a given application.
b. Allow time to expose the user's personnel to relevant techniques.
c. Allow for well-controlled changes in user requirements
d. Allow for reviews and GO-NOGO decisions after each design phase.

Only by a breakdown of the development effort into well-defined and clearly separate units can the problems of change be met.

5. An integrated set of standards must form the foundation for controlling the entire software development effort.

To acquire and maintain control, management must have the tools to impose a strict discipline at the very beginning. Strict standards are the key to this discipline. Typical standards include

a. *Project Definition.* These standards specify the form for stating the objectives, constraints, and overall project plan.
b. *System Specification.* These standards focus on complete specifications of system characteristics.
c. *Documentation.* These standards must focus on complete specifications of system characteristics. The standards should ensure that all documents are self-contained and easily read.
d. *Programming.* Generally these standards cover style, structure, and internal documentation of programs. Strict rules on the use of procedures, spacing and indentation, control structures, and choice of variable names are especially important. The ideal place to enforce these standards is the language compiler. Barring that, program reading by managers and programmers is a good alternative.
e. *Testing and Quality Control.* Prior to coding, standard procedures must be

established on developing test data and the buildup to a full cycle test. Good procedures for system modification and maintenance of the external documentation set must also be established prior to coding.

The Incremental Approach

We next outline an approach to the building of large systems that is based on the above premises. This approach, called the "Incremental Method," is due to Cave [Ref. C1]. It is incremental in the following senses:

a. It dictates a multiphase (not a single-phase) design effort.
b. Resources are committed on an incremental basis.
c. There are a series of clearly delineated review points.

Each phase follows a highly structured pattern of plan, do, write, and review.

Phase 1: Development of Project Objectives

The first phase is an explicit study of user objectives by the project management. Frequent contacts must be made with the user to develop a clear understanding of user problems. Emphasis must be placed on extracting relevant problem concerns and the elimination of arbitrary constraints that can only hamper further development. Hardware and software constraints must also be resolved. The result of this phase is a written description of user objectives. At this phase, it may not be possible to estimate the entire system development costs. At the very least, a careful estimate must be made to determine the cost of the next phase.

Finally, both the user and developer must allow ample time to review the proposed objectives. If further development effort is justified, then the next phase can be executed.

Phase 2: Functional Specification

This phase focuses on a detailed analysis of user requirements. The result of this phase is a set of documents that functionally defines the entire system as seen by the user. We believe that this definition should be so complete that the specifications will ultimately serve as a basis for the user documentation.

In sharp contrast with many conventional system development procedures, this phase is precisely the time to prepare user manuals. It is unwise to proceed further without giving the ultimate user a detailed idea of what to expect from the proposed system. It is certainly easier to change an unsatisfactory design during this phase, rather than after coding.

Finally, a complete review must be undertaken to decide if the detailed specification is still acceptable to the user and still feasible from the viewpoint of the system designer.

Phase 3: Environmental Specification

This phase is a period for determining environment requirements, such as equipment configurations, languages, and support software.

The first consideration should be a review of the existing technology. Trade-offs to meet the functional specification must be resolved. Any severe constraints on the hardware, support software, or operating system must be recognized. If the existing operating system or hardware requires major changes, then the cost of necessary changes must be defined.

The second concern should be the resolution of critical problems for which research or development is needed. Typical of such problems would be the development of unusual operating system algorithms or the design of a critical data structure for information storage and retrieval. Failure to resolve these problems early may undermine the success of the entire proposed system independently of the overall design approach.

Finally, a careful review should be undertaken to assess all required technical support. Any detected deficiencies in the hardware, operating system, or software support must be accounted for. Costs in time, people, and money should be estimated. Again, a GO-NOGO decision must be made by user and designer in concert.

Phase 4: System Design

This phase is devoted to detailed program documentation of the entire system and a matching of the design with effective personnel. The required programming personnel must first be given responsibility for documenting (before coding!) any proposed code. The procedures for doing this lie in the hands of the technical management. Each required document must be acceptable to management with full regard to the detailed functional specification standards.

It is important to stress the integration of individual involvement with the overall system documentation. Strict quality control must be placed on the system documentation from this point on. Poor individual documentation will be a likely predictor of poor code, and any such low-quality performance must be detected early. Any functional changes resulting from this phase must be incorporated in the design specifications themselves.

Finally again, the review. A review at this point is critical, for significant software costs will be involved if progress to the next phase is agreed upon.

Phase 5: System Construction

This phase is primarily concerned with writing and testing the programs for the system. Because of the rather elaborate preparation of the previous phases, this phase should proceed more smoothly and accurately than would generally be expected. The first major concern is the adoption of strict programming standards. The standards should include the choice of a high-level language, programming techniques, restrictions on program spacing and indentation, control structures, and the organization of programming teams.

The second major concern is a strict scheduling of program assignments and the required hardware facilities. It is all too easy to accumulate day-by-day slippage due to improper coordination of program writing and hardware test facilities.

Formal modification procedures must be developed to process corrections, refinements, or user requests for changes. Continuous maintenance and "shakedown" of all the programming documentation is vital to the integrity of the whole design effort. Loss of control over this activity can only lead to a slow but steady erosion of product quality.

Finally, management and the user must make a GO-NOGO decision to field the system. If agreement is reached, that is the next phase.

Phase 6: Real Environment Testing

During this period, the entire system is subjected to full-scale use under a simulated real user environment. The objective is the development of a full-cycle test whose effectiveness is satisfactory to both user and developer.

Representative user personnel are trained to use the system and to shake down the user's documentation. Formal modification procedures must be developed to process requests for corrections, refinements, and enhancements.

As the testing nears completion, detailed plans for the next phase, live operation, must be prepared. It is all too easy to let this planning fall by the wayside, but ultimately the user will have to live with the system. Planning should at least include cost estimates for steady state operation, and recovery procedures in case of system failure.

Finally, the user and developer must make the final GO-NOGO decision on whether to put the system into live operation or to return to make changes.

Phase 7: Live Operation

If the preceding phases have been properly completed, live operation will be easily effected.

Formal procedures to determine responsibility for possible system errors and the corresponding correction process must be developed. The system maintenance agent as well as the user should be able to initiate correction requests. Formal procedures for processing requests for system refinements and enhancements must also be developed. If there are multiple systems in the field, these procedures must preserve the system identity and the integrity of the documentation. To reduce total documentation and program modification efforts, it may be desirable to accumulate modification requests as long as the system remains operable.

Last, the user and developer should periodically review the entire effort. The level and formality of reviews will, of course, vary. In any event, formal user/designer reviews should take place annually at a minimum.

Conclusions

There are no simple techniques for developing large programs of high quality. What we do maintain, however, is that there are viable management guidelines for acquiring and maintaining project control. These guidelines can be backed up by a clean breakdown of projects into distinct phases and a set of strict standards.

One important point must be noted. The crucial parameter for measuring project success is user satisfaction. However, when overall user requirements cause estimates of time, people, or funding to exceed imposed constraints, it is necessary that a decision be made to either relax the requirements or halt the project! The decision to continue a project under uncertain estimates of required costs definitely places the responsibility for possible excess on management's shoulders. It is, therefore, essential that any method for management control must allow for periodic continuation decisions so that halts can ensure a minimum waste of resources.

One of the initial difficulties of the approach given here is the notion of "front-end loading," or the rather large involvement with the early noncoding stages of a project. This concept is initially hard to accept. Especially under an incremental funding arrangement, it appears that the user is paying a high price in the beginning and getting little return. However, when the detailed documentation is completed (the end of the functional specification phase), users are generally enthusiastic about the approach.

SOME PARTING COMMENTS

We would like to close this final chapter with a variety of thoughts on the notion of software quality. These thoughts have been partially expressed in previous chapters. They are neither new nor rigorously supported, but they do sum up a number of important issues.

Programmers are faced with numerous difficult problems. One point often confused is the difference between problem solving and programming. "Problem solving" can be viewed as the act of developing an algorithm to solve a given problem, "programming" as the act of transforming an algorithm into the linguistic concepts of a given programming language. In its conception, this book is primarily about programming, not problem solving. The techniques discussed in it will not necessarily help the programmer find a more efficient method of sorting, a faster method for computing Fourier Transforms, or a better heuristic for a chess-playing program.

The programmer's task is usually an intricate combination of both problem solving and programming. The issues in problem solving are vital to writing effective computer programs. Yet it is now well recognized that the "programming" of a given algorithm is far from trivial, and that the programmer should use all the available techniques of programming to ensure that his devised algorithm is clear. While good programming techniques will offer strong guidelines for the development of a good solution to a problem, we must admit that "programming," as conceived here, is only part of the programmer's task.

As mentioned in this chapter, the use of program flowcharts has been avoided in this text. As a method of program design, program flowcharts have been highly overvalued. The top-down approach to programming suppresses the use of these flowcharts in favor of highlighting a functional or procedural approach to program design. The case against program flowcharts is similar to the case against the GOTO. The lines and arrows can easily lead the user into a highly sequential mode of thinking. Furthermore, there is a tendency to think that once a program flowchart has been designed, the programming process is just about complete. Unfortunately, this is seldom the case. The programmer would be well-advised to try another approach whenever he or she thinks a program flowchart is needed.

Consider the Kriegspiel program of Chapter 3. In this program no complete module requires a listing of more than two pages of text, and most modules fit on a single page. This characteristic results from human engineering. We all know how difficult it can be to follow a long program. In any lengthy program, we usually try to abstract a logical portion of it that will give us an indication of its overall computation. Every programmer should recognize this fact and write each program so that each logical unit is clearly isolated on a page or two. Furthermore, as mentioned above, each unit should be definable in terms of simple input/output coordinates, avoiding the excessive use of global variables, for these can easily destroy the real modularity of logical units.

One underestimated problem in programming is that of keeping to language standards. Admittedly, our languages are so diffuse in scope and often so lacking in transparent linguistic features that it is hard not to introduce or use features that make up for some of the shortcomings. For example, the lack of better looping structures deserves remedy. Yet if we are to insist that programs are to be portable or that users can understand the programs written in other implementations, then we must stick to language features that are common to most (if not all) implementations. Even in writing a book such as this, the problem of keeping to a "standard" was difficult. Despite the difficulty, two points are worth mentioning. We should encourage the development of *more* and *better* standard definitions, and unless there is a compelling reason to do otherwise, we should adhere to the standards we have.

In recent years three notable efforts have occurred in the attempt to provide a significantly more effective, widely accepted computer language. The PL/1 language was introduced with the hope that it would soon become familiar to most programmers and replace its predecessor, FORTRAN. Unfortunately, PL/1 is so complex that it is difficult to learn and to implement at a low cost. The ALGOL 68 language was introduced in the attempt to eliminate the shortcomings of ALGOL 60 and to introduce important new linguistic concepts. The ALGOL 68 effort has been plagued by an overly complex definition and the lack of wider participation in its design. The recent effort to develop a new standard FOR-TRAN aims at a more powerful direct successor to FORTRAN IV. This effort is unfortunately hampered by the desire to be upwardly compatible with the existing definition of FORTRAN IV.

Of course, PASCAL itself has become widespread, although its acceptance in industry is certainly less than its acceptance in university circles. Finally, there are soundings from the Department of Defense on its proposal for a new common language. Despite all these notable attempts, it appears that it will be some years before a well-structured, mathematically sound and easily learnable new language becomes commonplace.

As regards PASCAL, there are three features to which we take strong objection. First is its inability to declare and initialize constant structures. In the Kriegspiel program presented earlier, we had severe problems of this sort. Notice the lengthy and uninspiring code to initialize the legal next move mappings. How nice to have had even a simple DATA statement as in FORTRAN.

Second, PASCAL's use of scalars is limited, since user-defined (enumerated) scalar names cannot be input or output from a program. While it is nice to say a type includes RED, WHITE, and BLUE, you must input them in some other form, normally an integer, and internally convert these values into colors.

Third, the absence of a "break" character makes it very difficult to interpret long names. How nice it would be to use names like X-COORDI-NATE, NEXT-SQUARE, or NUM-VALUES-READ. Trying to undo these long names when written without a break character is a time-consuming and unrewarding task. We strongly urge that future versions of PASCAL allow the longer names to be punctuated by an appropriate break character.

There are many other issues that need to be investigated. Among these are the need for better documentation of programs, better programming languages, the establishment of problem definition techniques, the development of a more manageable succesor to PASCAL, and the promotion of human factors.

The final issue is the critical need to upgrade the entire programming effort.

With all of the new interest in programming, progress is certainly on its way. We must discipline ourselves to this interest but only adopt what is really progressive. Perhaps the best motivation is to recall how much hard work went into the last program you wrote and also that the program you write today may be the program you will maintain next year.

EXERCISES

Exercise 5.1   (Use Mnemonic Identifiers)

In considering the creation of the proper psychological set for identifiers, the programmer must guard against using identifiers whose relationships with their values is vague, tenuous, or peculiar to the programmer himself. The purpose of the following program segment has been obscured by the use of mnemonic identifiers and intermediate variables that appear reasonable at first glance but that are in fact misleading and confusing. State the purpose of this segment. What quantity is represented by "INTER"? Rewrite the segment using a better choice of mnemonic identifiers and intermediate variables.

```
VAR
    DENOM, SLOPE, INTER: REAL;
    ROW, COL, NUM       :  INTEGER;
    A                   :  ARRAY[1..2, 1..2] OF REAL;



BEGIN

    FOR ROW := 1 TO 2 DO
        FOR COL := 1 TO 2 DO
            READLN(A[I,J]);

    IF A[1,1] = A[2,2]
        THEN
            WRITELN('NO VALUE')
        ELSE
            BEGIN

                NUM    := A[1,2] - A[2,2];
                DENOM  := A[1,1] - A[2,1];
                SLOPE  := NUM / DENOM;
                INTER  := A[1,2] - SLOPE * A[1,1];

                WRITELN('THE ANSWER IS ', INTER)

            END

END
```

Exercise 5.2   (Use of Psychologically "Distant" Identifiers)

Consider the following program specification:

Input: three pairs of integers denoting the co-ordinates of three points on a grid.

Output: the area of the triangle defined by the three points.

Write such a program using *only* the identifiers X1, X2, X3, . . .

Exercise 5.3   (Global Variables in Functions)

What is printed by the following piece of code?

```
VAR
    A: INTEGER;


FUNCTION G(X: INTEGER): INTEGER;

BEGIN

    A := 2 * (X + 1);
    G := A

END;

FUNCTION F(X: INTEGER): INTEGER;

BEGIN

    A := X + G(X);
    F := 2 * A

END;


BEGIN

    A := 1;
    A := F(F(2)) + A;

    WRITELN(A)

END
```

Exercise 5.4

It is likely that you disagree strongly with at least one of the topics discussed in this chapter. Pick the one that you disagree with the most and prepare a comprehensive counterproposal. After the customary number of rewrites, have someone else read it. (Hint: Choose a friend to do the reading.) When you are finished, send the results to the authors of this book.

Exercise 5.5

This exercise is for those who have just completed reading our brief text. First, we want to thank you for the compliment of reading this book. Second, compare the style of the next program you write with one you wrote prior to reading our book. Evaluate the impact of our book on your programming style and send us a letter.

Exercise 5.6

Below are two advanced topics that we would have liked to discuss in this chapter. Pick the one that interests you the most, discuss the relevant issues, seek out the opinions of others, and present proposals which resolve some of the problems therein. Submit your results to a conference:

Topic 1: "The Problem with Problem Definition"

Issues: How should one detail inputs and outputs? What is a "functional" specification? What constitutes a "complete" definition? How much of a definition can be used for documentation? Where do implementation requirements go? What about condition-action lists versus decision tables? How should the layout and organization of a good, complete definition appear?

Topic 2: "The Global Variable Problem"

Issues: Should PASCAL limit the use of global variables? What changes would you make in PASCAL to encourage better isolation of modules.

Exercise 5.7

There once was a frog named Mr. Croak who was beset with three daughters of marriageable age, Ribbit1, Ribbit2, and Ribbit3. Now the only eligible male frog, Horatio, fell for Ribbit2 and proceeded to ask for her leg in marriage. However, Mr. Croak, concerned with the marriage prospects for Ribbit1 and Ribbit3, proposed the following: Whichever one of his daughters leaped the farthest would become Horatio's wife. Now, Horatio knew, but Mr. Croak didn't, that Ribbit1 could jump three lily pads, that Ribbit2 could jump twice as far as Ribbit1, and that Ribbit3 could jump only one third as far as Ribbit2. Thus Horatio readily agreed and persuaded Mr. Croak that the following computer program should determine who would wed him. (Note: HEIGHTRIB1, HEIGHTRIB2, and HEIGHTRIB3 denote the heights of the jumps of Ribbits, 1, 2, and 3.

```
VAR
    JUMPRIB1, JUMPRIB2, JUMPRIB3: REAL;


FUNCTION F(X: REAL): REAL;

BEGIN

    X := 2 * X;
    F := X

END;


FUNCTION G(X: REAL): REAL;

BEGIN

    X := (1/3) * X;
    G := X

END;
```

```
BEGIN

    HEIGHTRIB1 := 3;
    HEIGHTRIB2 := F(HEIGHTRIB1);
    HEIGHTRIB3 := G(HEIGHTRIB2);

    WRITELN('RIBBIT1 = ', HEIGHTRIB1,
             RIBBIT2 = ', HEIGHTRIB2,
             RIBBIT3 = ', HEIGHTRIB3)

END
```

What is the moral of the story?

Exercise 5.8

Take the rest of the afternoon off. (We knew we could use this somewhere.)

APPENDIX

APPENDIX A

Summary of Program Standards

General Requirements

[GEN-1] Any violation of the program standards must be approved by someone appointed to enforce the standards.

[GEN-2] For each installation and for each application, there should be an adopted set of standard user-defined names.

[GEN-3] Each installation shall have established alignment (prettyprinting) conventions.

[GEN-4] No program unit may exceed two pages of code.

[GEN-5] All programs shall include the following comment:

```
(*   **   PROGRAM TITLE          Brief title                  *)
(*   **
(*   **   WRITTEN BY             Name of author(s)            *)
(*   **   DATE WRITTEN           Date of first compilation    *)
(*   **   WRITTEN FOR            Responsible unit             *)
(*   **
(*   **   PROGRAM SUMMARY        Brief program summary        *)
               .
               .
               .
(*   **   INPUT AND OUTPUT FILES
(*           file name           Brief description of use     *)
               .
               .
               .
```

Declarations

[DCL-1] All scalars that remain constant throughout a program must be specified in a constant declaration.

[DCL-2] Each program must have a (possibly empty) set of global variables selected by some designated person before any code is written. These are the only variables that can be used globally.

[DCL-3] No function may alter any of its actual parameters or change the value of any global variable.

[DCL-4] The parameters of a procedure must be declared with comments describing the logical role of each parameter. For example,

PROCEDURE EXAMPLE

```
(   (* IN *)        A, B:      INTEGER;
    (* IN OUT *)   VAR C,D:   INTEGER;
    (* OUT *)      VAR E,F:   REAL;  )
```

The comments (* IN *), (* IN OUT *), and (* OUT *) may be replaced by more informative comments. For example: (* USING *), (* UPDATING *), and (* GIVING *).

[DCL-5] The end of each procedure or function declaration must be followed by a comment giving the procedure or function name. For example: END (* EXAMPLE *).

Control Structures

[CNTRL-1] GOTOs are not allowed.

[CNTRL-2] Nesting of any combination of IF, FOR, WHILE, CASE, and RE-PEAT statements must be no more than four levels deep. An exception is allowed for simulating a generalized case statement.

[CNTRL-3] The end of a case statement must be followed by the comment END (*CASE*).

[CNTRL-4] Null statements must include a comment line like (* DO NOTHING *).

APPENDIX B

Pascal Prettyprinting Standards

General Rules

[GEN-1] The spacing of any construct not specifically mentioned in this standard is left open to the user. The user may (and is encouraged to) insert extra spaces and extra blank lines beyond those given in this standard to promote readability.

[GEN-2] Each statement must begin on a separate line.

[GEN-3] Each line shall be less than or equal to 72 characters.

[GEN-4] Comments that are appended at the end of a line of code and that are continued on successive lines must be written so that continued lines are under the initial comment fragment.

[GEN-5] The keywords REPEAT, BEGIN, END, and RECORD must stand on a line by themselves (or possibly followed by supporting comments).

[GEN-6] At least one blank line must appear before LABEL, CONST, TYPE, and VAR declarations; at least three blank lines must appear before PROCEDURE and FUNCTION declarations.

[GEN-7] At least one space must appear before and after ':=', and '='. At least one space must appear after ':'. At least one space must appear before and after '*' in a comment.

Alignment Rules

[ALIGN-1] PROGRAM, PROCEDURE, and FUNCTION headings must begin at the left margin.

[ALIGN-2] The main BEGIN-END block for a program, procedure, or function shall be lined up with the corresponding heading.

[ALIGN-3] Each statement within a BEGIN-END, REPEAT-UNTIL, or CASE statement must be aligned.

Indentation Rules

[INDENT-1]   The bodies of LABEL, CONST, TYPE, and VAR declarations must be indented from the beginning of the corresponding header keywords.

[INDENT-2]   The bodies of BEGIN-END, FOR, REPEAT, WHILE, WITH, and CASE statements, as well as the bodies of RECORD-END structures, must be indented from their corresponding header keywords.

[INDENT-3]   An IF-THEN-ELSE statement must be displayed as:

```
IF expression
   THEN
         statement
   ELSE
         statement
```

or

```
   IF expression THEN
      statement
   ELSE
      statement
```

An exception is allowed for simulating a generalized case statement:

```
IF expression₁ THEN
      statement₁
ELSE IF expression₂ THEN
      statement₂
              .
              .
              .

ELSE
         statementₙ
```

An Automatic Formatting Program for PASCAL

PASCAL, like many languages, is a "free-format" language in that there are no column-position or line-boundary restrictions on statements, declarations, or comments. Free-format languages have the advantage that the programmer may format his code in any way that well reflects the logical structuring of his program. Unfortunately, such languages also have the disadvantage that the programmer may just as easily impose no logical formatting scheme whatsoever. A program that is poorly formatted is often hard to maintain and modify; its poor readability may lead only to confusion. In order to alleviate this problem, we have attempted to develop a set of useful formatting standards for PASCAL here. A program that has been thoughtfully formatted according to a set of such standards is said to be *prettyprinted* (see example in the following pages).

Imposing formatting restrictions necessarily imposes a burden on a programmer, particularly on a student programmer, since he must keypunch or type in the entire program himself. It is therefore useful to have a facility for taking arbitrarily formatted source code and automatically prettyprinting it. However, the design of any such prettyprinter must deal with several serious issues.

Typically, automatic prettyprinters use a heavy hand in formatting a program, right down to every last semicolon. Such a scheme either formats everything in a rigid fashion, which is bound to be displeasing, or else it provides the programmer with a voluminous set of "options." Furthermore, such a scheme must do a full syntax analysis on the program, which means that it falls prey to the bane of all compilers: error recovery. Thus, before a program may be prettyprinted, it must be completely written and debugged. If the programmer wishes to prettyprint a program still under development, he is out of luck, or else he must do it by hand, in which case he has no need for an automatic prettyprinter when he is done.

We believe that it is not necessary to impose more than a *minimum* set of restrictions and that any prettyprinter should yield to the programmer's discretion beyond this minimum. No matter how many options a prettyprinter has, it cannot possibly have one to please everyone in every possible case. We further believe that a prettyprinter should not commit itself to a full syntax analysis. It should only do prettyprinting on a local basis, dealing with individual constructs rather than entire programs.

In order to demonstrate these assertions, we have designed and implemented, in PASCAL, just such a prettyprinter. Intended mostly as an editing aid, it thus does not include most of the "kitchen sink" facilities used by other prettyprinters. It simply rearranges the spacing and identation of certain constructs in order to make the logical structure of a program more visually apparent. Furthermore, the prettyprinter forces only a minimum amount of spacing and indentation where those are needed. Any extra spaces or blank lines found in the program beyond the required minimum are left there. This approach leaves the programmer a good deal of flexibility for use as he sees fit.

The general strategy of the prettyprinter is simply to scan the program on a symbol-by-symbol basis, keeping track of the amount of space found between each symbol. If a distinguished symbol (such as "BEGIN," "UNTIL," etc.) is found, a table is consulted to see if any special prettyprinting actions are associated with that symbol. The most important actions are the indentation and de-indentation of the left margin, since they are the most difficult to handle. They are difficult because the prettyprinter needs more than local information to determine how and when to de-indent the margin. These decisions are accomplished through the use of a stack. Each time the margin is indented, the symbol causing indentation is placed on the stack along with the previous position of the left margin. Thus, when de-indentation is called for, all that is needed is to pop the stack in order to determine what position the margin is to be restored to.

Since prettyprinting is done purely on a symbol-by-symbol basis, no snytax analysis is needed, and the program to be prettyprinted need not be syntactically correct. In fact, it need not even be a complete program. All that is required is that each individual construct be complete ("BEGINs" must have their "ENDs", "REPEATs" their "UNTILs", and so on). Furthermore, no error recovery is needed, since no errors are possible in the absence of a syntax analysis. An ill-defined construct may lead to ill-defined prettyprinting, but such errors are far from subtle and are easy to correct.

As an example of the prettyprinter's performance, consider the following program fragment:

```
TYPE SCALE=(CENTIGRADE, FAHRENHEIT);
FUNCTION CONVERT ( DEGREES : INTEGER;
                        NEWSCALE: SCALE   ) : INTEGER;
BEGIN IF NEWSCALE=CENTIGRADE THEN
```

```
CONVERT:=ROUND((9/5*DEGREES) +32) ELSE
CONVERT:=ROUND(5/9*(DEGREE-32)) END;
```

When fed into the prettyprinter, the following output results:

```
TYPE SCALE = (CENTIGRADE, FAHRENHEIT);
FUNCTION CONVERT( DEGREES : INTEGER;
                       NEWSCALE: SCALE  ) :      INTEGER;
BEGIN
    IF NEWSCALE=CENTIGRADE
       THEN
            CONVERT :=  ROUND((9/5*DEGREES) +32)
       ELSE
            CONVERT :=  ROUND(5/9*(DEGREES-32))
END;
```

(Note that some care was taken to format the function header in a special way and that the prettyprinter did not interfere.)

The prettyprinter that we have implemented is written entirely in standard PASCAL [W3] and should compile and run using any PASCAL compiler. We have compiled it using the PASCAL 6000-3.4 compiler from Zurich and run it using 11K (octal) of core on our CDC CYBER 74.

Since the program as written is highly modularized and table-driven, it is extremely easy to modify and upgrade. Our concern for proper abstraction leads to a certain amount of runtime overhead. Therefore, the program runs marginally slower than the PASCAL compiler. Execution speed could be increased considerably by making most of the variables global and by eliminating some of the procedures and inserting them inline. We feel, however, that the tradeoff is not worth it.

JON F. HUERAS
HENRY F. LEDGARD

```
(*=============================================================================*)
(*                                                                             *)
(*    PROGRAM TITLE: PASCAL PRETTYPRINTING PROGRAM                             *)
(*                                                                             *)
(*    AUTHORS:  JON F. HUERAS AND HENRY F. LEDGARD                             *)
(*              COMPUTER AND INFORMATION SCIENCE DEPARTMENT                     *)
(*              UNIVERSITY OF MASSACHUSETTS, AMHERST                            *)
(*              (EARLIER VERSIONS AND CONTRIBUTIONS BY RANDY CHOW              *)
(*               AND JOHN GORMAN. )                                            *)
(*                                                                             *)
(*    PROGRAM SUMMARY:                                                         *)
(*                                                                             *)
(*       THIS PROGRAM TAKES AS INPUT A PASCAL PROGRAM AND                      *)
(*       REFORMATS THE PROGRAM ACCORDING TO A STANDARD SET OF                  *)
(*       PRETTYPRINTING RULES. THE PRETTYPRINTED PROGRAM IS GIVEN              *)
(*       AS OUTPUT.   THE PRETTYPRINTING RULES ARE GIVEN BELOW.                *)
(*                                                                             *)
(*       AN IMPORTANT FEATURE IS THE PROVISION FOR THE USE OF EXTRA            *)
(*       SPACES AND EXTRA BLANK LINES.   THEY MAY BE FREELY INSERTED BY        *)
(*       THE USER IN ADDITION TO THE SPACES AND BLANK LINES INSERTED           *)
(*.      BY THE PRETTYPRINTER.                                                 *)
(*                                                                             *)
(*       NO ATTEMPT IS MADE TO DETECT OR CORRECT SYNTACTIC ERRORS IN           *)
(*       THE USER'S PROGRAM.   HOWEVER, SYNTACTIC ERRORS MAY RESULT IN         *)
(*       ERRONEOUS PRETTYPRINTING.                                            *)
(*                                                                             *)
(*                                                                             *)
(*    INPUT FILE:  INPUTFILE     - A FILE OF CHARACTERS, PRESUMABLY A          *)
(*                                 PASCAL PROGRAM OR PROGRAM FRAGMENT.          *)
(*                                                                             *)
(*    OUTPUT FILES: OUTPUTFILE - THE PRETTYPRINTED PROGRAM.                    *)
(*                                                                             *)
(*                   OUTPUT     - STANDARD PASCAL FILE FOR RUNTIME             *)
(*                                MESSAGES.                                    *)
(*                                                                             *)
(*=============================================================================*)
```

```
(*==========================================================================*)
(*                                                                          *)
(*                     PASCAL PRETTYPRINTING RULES                          *)
(*                                                                          *)
(*                                                                          *)
(*   [ GENERAL PRETTYPRINTING RULES ]                                       *)
(*                                                                          *)
(*   1.   ANY SPACES OR BLANK LINES BEYOND THOSE GENERATED BY THE           *)
(*        PRETTYPRINTER ARE LEFT ALONE.   THE USER IS ENCOURAGED, FOR THE   *)
(*        SAKE OF READABILITY, TO MAKE USE OF THIS FACILITY.                *)
(*           IN ADDITION, COMMENTS ARE LEFT WHERE THEY ARE FOUND, UNLESS    *)
(*        THEY ARE SHIFTED RIGHT BY PRECEEDING TEXT ON A LINE.              *)
(*                                                                          *)
(*   2.   ALL STATEMENTS AND DECLARATIONS BEGIN ON SEPARATE LINES.          *)
(*                                                                          *)
(*   3.   NO LINE MAY BE GREATER THAN 72 CHARACTERS LONG.   ANY LINE        *)
(*        LONGER THAN THIS IS CONTINUED ON A SEPARATE LINE.                 *)
(*                                                                          *)
(*   4.   THE KEYWORDS "BEGIN", "END", "REPEAT", AND "RECORD" ARE           *)
(*        FORCED TO STAND ON LINES BY THEMSELVES (OR POSSIBLY FOLLWED BY    *)
(*        SUPPORTING COMMENTS).                                             *)
(*           IN  ADDITION, THE "UNTIL" CLAUSE OF A "REPEAT-UNTIL" STATE-    *)
(*        MENT IS FORCED TO START ON A NEW LINE.                            *)
(*                                                                          *)
(*   5.   A BLANK LINE IS FORCED BEFORE THE KEYWORDS "PROGRAM",             *)
(*        "PROCEDURE", "FUNCTION", "LABEL", "CONST", "TYPE", AND "VAR".     *)
(*                                                                          *)
(*   6.   A SPACE IS FORCED BEFORE AND AFTER THE SYMBOLS ":=" AND           *)
(*        "=".  ADDITIONALLY, A SPACE IS FORCED AFTER THE SYMBOL ":".       *)
(*                                                                          *)
(*                                                                          *)
(*   [ INDENTATION RULES ]                                                  *)
(*                                                                          *)
(*   1.   THE BODIES OF "LABEL", "CONST", "TYPE", AND "VAR" DECLARA-        *)
(*        TIONS ARE INDENTED FROM THEIR CORRESPONDING DECLARATION HEADER    *)
(*        KEYWORDS.                                                         *)
(*                                                                          *)
(*   2.   THE BODIES OF "BEGIN-END", "REPEAT-UNTIL", "FOR", "WHILE",        *)
(*        "WITH", AND "CASE" STATEMENTS, AS WELL AS "RECORD-END" STRUC-     *)
(*        TURES AND "CASE" VARIANTS (TO ONE LEVEL) ARE INDENTED FROM        *)
(*        THEIR HEADER KEYWORDS.                                            *)
(*                                                                          *)
(*   3.   AN "IF-THEN-ELSE" STATEMENT IS INDENTED AS FOLLOWS:               *)
(*                                                                          *)
(*            IF <EXPRESSION>                                               *)
(*                THEN                                                      *)
(*                    <STATEMENT>                                           *)
(*                ELSE                                                      *)
(*                    <STATEMENT>                                           *)
(*                                                                          *)
(*                                                                          *)
(*==========================================================================*)
```

```
(*==================================================================*)
(*                                                                  *)
(*                       GENERAL ALGORITHM                          *)
(*                                                                  *)
(*                                                                  *)
(*     THE STRATEGY OF THE PRETTYPRINTER IS TO SCAN SYMBOLS FROM    *)
(*  THE INPUT PROGRAM AND MAP EACH SYMBOL INTO A PRETTYPRINTING     *)
(*  ACTION, INDEPENDENTLY OF THE CONTEXT IN WHICH THE SYMBOL        *)
(*  APPEARS.   THIS IS ACCOMPLISHED BY A TABLE OF PRETTYPRINTING    *)
(*  OPTIONS.                                                        *)
(*                                                                  *)
(*     FOR EACH DISTINGUISHED SYMBOL IN THE TABLE, THERE IS AN      *)
(*  ASSOCIATED SET OF OPTIONS.   IF THE OPTION HAS BEEN SELECTED FOR*)
(*  THE SYMBOL BEING SCANNED, THEN THE ACTION CORRESPONDING WITH    *)
(*  EACH OPTION IS PERFORMED.                                       *)
(*                                                                  *)
(*     THE BASIC ACTIONS INVOLVED IN PRETTYPRINTING ARE THE INDENT- *)
(*  ATION AND DE-INDENTATION OF THE MARGIN.   EACH TIME THE MARGIN IS*)
(*  INDENTED, THE PREVIOUS VALUE OF THE MARGIN IS PUSHED ONTO A     *)
(*  STACK, ALONG WITH THE NAME OF THE SYMBOL THAT CAUSED IT TO BE   *)
(*  INDENTED.   EACH TIME THE MARGIN IS DE-INDENTED, THE STACK IS   *)
(*  POPPED OFF TO OBTAIN THE PREVIOUS VALUE OF THE MARGIN.          *)
(*                                                                  *)
(*     THE PRETTYPRINTING OPTIONS ARE PROCESSED IN THE FOLLOWING    *)
(*  ORDER, AND INVOKE THE FOLLOWING ACTIONS:                        *)
(*                                                                  *)
(*                                                                  *)
(*     CRSUPPRESS         - IF A CARRIAGE RETURN HAS BEEN INSERTED  *)
(*                           FOLLOWING THE PREVIOUS SYMBOL, THEN IT IS*)
(*                           INHIBITED UNTIL THE NEXT SYMBOL IS PRINTED.*)
(*                                                                  *)
(*     CRBEFORE          - A CARRIAGE RETURN IS INSERTED BEFORE THE *)
(*                           CURRENT SYMBOL (UNLESS ONE IS ALREADY THERE)*)
(*                                                                  *)
(*     BLANKLINEBEFORE - A BLANK LINE IS INSERTED BEFORE THE CURRENT*)
(*                           SYMBOL (UNLESS ALREADY THERE).         *)
(*                                                                  *)
(*     DINDENTONKEYS     - IF ANY OF THE SPECIFIED KEYS ARE ON TOP OF*)
(*                           OF THE STACK, THE STACK IS POPPED, DE-INDEN-*)
(*                           TING THE MARGIN.   THE PROCESS IS REPEATED*)
(*                           UNTIL THE TOP OF THE STACK IS NOT ONE OF THE*)
(*                           SPECIFIED KEYS.                        *)
(*                                                                  *)
(*     DINDENT            - THE STACK IS UNCONDITIONALLY POPPED AND THE*)
(*                           MARGIN IS DE-INDENTED.                 *)
(*                                                                  *)
(*     SPACEBEFORE       - A SPACE IS INSERTED BEFORE THE SYMBOL BEING*)
(*                           SCANNED (UNLESS ALREADY THERE).        *)
(*                                                                  *)
(*  [ THE SYMBOL IS PRINTED AT THIS POINT ]                         *)
(*                                                                  *)
(*     SPACEAFTER        - A SPACE IS INSERTED AFTER THE SYMBOL BEING*)
(*                           SCANNED (UNLESS ALREADY THERE).        *)
(*                                                                  *)
(*     GOBBLESYMBOLS     - SYMBOLS ARE CONTINUOUSLY SCANNED AND PRINTED*)
(*                           WITHOUT ANY PROCESSING UNTIL ONE OF THE*)
(*                           SPECIFIED SYMBOLS IS SEEN (BUT NOT GOBBLED).*)
(*                                                                  *)
(*     INDENTBYTAB       - THE MARGIN IS INDENTED BY A STANDARD AMOUNT*)
(*                           FROM THE PREVIOUS MARGIN.              *)
(*                                                                  *)
(*     INDENTTOCLP       - THE MARGIN IS INDENTED TO THE CURRENT LINE*)
(*                           POSITION.                              *)
(*                                                                  *)
(*     CRAFTER           - A CARRIAGE RETURN IS INSERTED FOLLOWING THE*)
(*                           SYMBOL SCANNED.                        *)
(*==================================================================*)
```

```
PROGRAM PRETTYPRINT( (* FROM *)  INPUTFILE,
                     (* TO *)    OUTPUTFILE,
                     (* USING *) OUTPUT      );


CONST

      MAXSYMBOLSIZE = 200;  (* THE MAXIMUM SIZE (IN CHARACTERS) OF A    *)
                           (* SYMBOL SCANNED BY THE LEXICAL SCANNER.   *)

      MAXSTACKSIZE  = 100;  (* THE MAXIMUM NUMBER OF SYMBOLS CAUSING    *)
                           (* INDENTATION THAT MAY BE STACKED.         *)

      MAXKEYLENGTH  =  10;  (* THE MAXIMUM LENGTH (IN CHARACTERS) OF A *)
                           (* PASCAL RESERVED KEYWORD.                 *)
      MAXLINESIZE   =  72;  (* THE MAXIMUM SIZE (IN CHARACTERS) OF A    *)
                           (* LINE OUTPUT BY THE PRETTYPRINTER.        *)

      SLOWFAIL1     =  30;  (* UP TO THIS COLUMN POSITION, EACH TIME    *)
                           (* "INDENTBYTAB" IS INVOKED, THE MARGIN     *)
                           (* WILL BE INDENTED BY "INDENT1".           *)

      SLOWFAIL2     =  48;  (* UP TO THIS COLUMN POSITION, EACH TIME    *)
                           (* "INDENTBYTAB" IS INVOKED, THE MARGIN     *)
                           (* WILL BE INDENTED BY "INDENT2".  BEYOND   *)
                           (* THIS, NO INDENTATION OCCURS.             *)

      INDENT1       =   3;

      INDENT2       =   1;


      SPACE = ' ';
```

```
TYPE

     KEYSYMBOL = ( PROQSYM,      FUNCSYM,      PROCSYM,
                   LABELSYM,     CONSTSYM,     TYPESYM,      VARSYM,
                   BEGINSYM,     REPEATSYM,    RECORDSYM,
                   CASESYM,      CASEVARSYM,   OFSYM,
                   FORSYM,       WHILESYM,     WITHSYM,      DOSYM,
                   IFSYM,        THENSYM,      ELSESYM,
                   ENDSYM,       UNTILSYM,
                   BECOMES,      OPENCOMMENT,  CLOSECOMMENT,
                   SEMICOLON,    COLON,        EQUALS,
                   OPENPAREN,    CLOSEPAREN,   PERIOD,
                   ENDOFFILE,
                   OTHERSYM );

     OPTION = ( CRSUPPRESS,
                CRBEFORE,
                BLANKLINEBEFORE,
                DINDENTONKEYS,
                DINDENT,
                SPACEBEFORE,
                SPACEAFTER,
                GOBBLESYMBOLS,
                INDENTBYTAB,
                INDENTTOCLP,
                CRAFTER );

   OPTIONSET = SET OF OPTION;

   KEYSYMSET = SET OF KEYSYMBOL;

   TABLEENTRY = RECORD
                    OPTIONSSELECTED  : OPTIONSET;
                    DINDENTSYMBOLS   : KEYSYMSET;
                    GOBBLETERMINATORS: KEYSYMSET
                END;

   OPTIONTABLE = ARRAY [ KEYSYMBOL ] OF TABLEENTRY;
```

```
KEY = PACKED ARRAY [ 1..MAXKEYLENGTH ] OF CHAR;


KEYWORDTABLE = ARRAY [ PROGSYM..UNTILSYM ] OF KEY;


SPECIALCHAR = PACKED ARRAY [ 1..2 ] OF CHAR;

DBLCHRSET = SET OF BECOMES..OPENCOMMENT;

DBLCHARTABLE = ARRAY [ BECOMES..OPENCOMMENT ] OF SPECIALCHAR;

SGLCHARTABLE = ARRAY [ SEMICOLON..PERIOD ] OF CHAR;


STRING = ARRAY [ 1..MAXSYMBOLSIZE ] OF CHAR;

SYMBOL = RECORD
              NAME         : KEYSYMBOL;
              VALUE        : STRING;
              LENGTH       : INTEGER;
              SPACESBEFORE : INTEGER;
              CRSBEFORE    : INTEGER
         END;

SYMBOLINFO = ^SYMBOL;


CHARNAME = ( LETTER,    DIGIT,    BLANK,    QUOTE,
             ENDOFLINE, FILEMARK, OTHERCHAR          );

CHARINFO = RECORD
               NAME : CHARNAME;
               VALUE: CHAR
           END;


STACKENTRY = RECORD
                 INDENTSYMBOL: KEYSYMBOL;
                 PREVMARGIN  : INTEGER
             END;

SYMBOLSTACK = ARRAY [ 1..MAXSTACKSIZE ] OF STACKENTRY;
```

```
VAR

        INPUTFILE,
        OUTPUTFILE: TEXT;

        RECORDSEEN: BOOLEAN;

        CURRCHAR,
        NEXTCHAR: CHARINFO;

        CURRSYM,
        NEXTSYM: SYMBOLINFO;

        CRPENDING: BOOLEAN;

        PPOPTION: OPTIONTABLE;

        KEYWORD: KEYWORDTABLE;

        DBLCHARS: DBLCHRSET;

        DBLCHAR: DBLCHARTABLE;
        SGLCHAR: SGLCHARTABLE;

        STACK: SYMBOLSTACK;
        TOP  : INTEGER;

        CURRLINEPOS,
        CURRMARGIN :  INTEGER;
```

```
PROCEDURE GETCHAR( (* FROM *)        VAR INPUTFILE : TEXT;
                   (* UPDATING *)  VAR NEXTCHAR  : CHARINFO;
                   (* RETURNING *) VAR CURRCHAR  : CHARINFO );

BEGIN (* GETCHAR *)

   CURRCHAR := NEXTCHAR;

   WITH NEXTCHAR DO
      BEGIN

         IF EOF(INPUTFILE)
            THEN
               NAME  := FILEMARK

      ELSE IF EOLN(INPUTFILE)
            THEN
               NAME  := ENDOFLINE

      ELSE IF INPUTFILE^ IN ['A'..'Z']
            THEN
               NAME  := LETTER

      ELSE IF INPUTFILE^ IN ['0'..'9']
            THEN
               NAME  := DIGIT

      ELSE IF INPUTFILE^ = ''''
            THEN
               NAME  := QUOTE

      ELSE IF INPUTFILE^ = SPACE
            THEN
               NAME  := BLANK

      ELSE NAME := OTHERCHAR;

         IF NAME IN [ FILEMARK, ENDOFLINE ]
            THEN
               VALUE := SPACE
            ELSE
               VALUE := INPUTFILE^;

         IF NAME <> FILEMARK
            THEN
               GET(INPUTFILE)

      END (* WITH *)

END; (* GETCHAR *)
```

```
PROCEDURE STORENEXTCHAR( (* FROM *)              VAR INPUTFILE : TEXT;
                        (* UPDATING *)           VAR LENGTH    : INTEGER;
                                                 VAR CURRCHAR,
                                                     NEXTCHAR  : CHARINFO;
                        (* PLACING IN *)         VAR VALUE     : STRING   );

BEGIN (* STORENEXTCHAR *)

   GETCHAR( (* FROM *)          INPUTFILE,
            (* UPDATING *)      NEXTCHAR,
            (* RETURNING *)     CURRCHAR   );

   IF LENGTH < MAXSYMBOLSIZE
      THEN
         BEGIN

            LENGTH := LENGTH + 1;

            VALUE [LENGTH] := CURRCHAR. VALUE

         END

END; (* STORENEXTCHAR *)




PROCEDURE SKIPSPACES( (* IN *)            VAR INPUTFILE    : TEXT;
                      (* UPDATING *)      VAR CURRCHAR,
                                              NEXTCHAR     : CHARINFO;
                      (* RETURNING *)     VAR SPACESBEFORE,
                                              CRSBEFORE    : INTEGER  );

BEGIN (* SKIPSPACES *)

   CRSBEFORE      := O;

   WHILE NEXTCHAR. NAME IN [ BLANK, ENDOFLINE ] DO
      BEGIN

         GETCHAR( (* FROM *)          INPUTFILE,
                  (* UPDATING *)      NEXTCHAR,
                  (* RETURNING *)     CURRCHAR   );

         CASE CURRCHAR. NAME OF

            BLANK     : SPACESBEFORE := SPACESBEFORE + 1;

            ENDOFLINE : BEGIN
                           CRSBEFORE    := CRSBEFORE + 1;
                           SPACESBEFORE := O
                        END

         END (* CASE *)

      END (* WHILE *)

END; (* SKIPSPACES *)
```

```
PROCEDURE GETCOMMENT( (* FROM *)       VAR INPUTFILE : TEXT;
                      (* UPDATING *) VAR CURRCHAR,
                                         NEXTCHAR  : CHARINFO;
                                     VAR NAME      : KEYSYMBOL;
                                     VAR VALUE     : STRING;
                                     VAR LENGTH    : INTEGER   );

BEGIN (* GETCOMMENT *)

   NAME := OPENCOMMENT;

   WHILE NOT(    ((CURRCHAR.VALUE = '*') AND (NEXTCHAR.VALUE = ')'))
              OR (NEXTCHAR.NAME = ENDOFLINE)
              OR (NEXTCHAR.NAME = FILEMARK)) DO

       STORENEXTCHAR( (* FROM *)        INPUTFILE,
                      (* UPDATING *) LENGTH,
                                     CURRCHAR,
                                     NEXTCHAR,
                      (* IN *)       VALUE      );


   IF (CURRCHAR.VALUE = '*') AND (NEXTCHAR.VALUE = ')')
      THEN
         BEGIN

            STORENEXTCHAR( (* FROM *)        INPUTFILE,
                           (* UPDATING *) LENGTH,
                                          CURRCHAR,
                                          NEXTCHAR,
                           (* IN *)       VALUE      );

            NAME := CLOSECOMMENT

         END

END; (* GETCOMMENT *)
```

```
FUNCTION IDTYPE( (* OF *)          VALUE  : STRING;
                (* USING *)        LENGTH : INTEGER )
                (* RETURNING *)                       : KEYSYMBOL;

VAR
    I: INTEGER;

    KEYVALUE: KEY;

    HIT: BOOLEAN;

    THISKEY: KEYSYMBOL;


BEGIN (* IDTYPE *)

   IDTYPE := OTHERSYM;

   IF LENGTH <= MAXKEYLENGTH
      THEN
         BEGIN

            FOR I := 1 TO LENGTH DO
               KEYVALUE [I] := VALUE [I];

            FOR I := LENGTH+1 TO MAXKEYLENGTH DO
               KEYVALUE [I] := SPACE;

            THISKEY := PROGSYM;
            HIT     := FALSE;

            WHILE NOT(HIT OR (PRED(THISKEY) = UNTILSYM)) DO
               IF KEYVALUE = KEYWORD [THISKEY]
                  THEN
                     HIT := TRUE
                  ELSE
                     THISKEY := SUCC(THISKEY);

            IF HIT
               THEN
                  IDTYPE := THISKEY

         END;

END; (* IDTYPE *)
```

```
PROCEDURE GETIDENTIFIER( (* FROM *)       VAR INPUTFILE : TEXT;
                        (* UPDATING *)    VAR CURRCHAR,
                                              NEXTCHAR  : CHARINFO;
                        (* RETURNING *)   VAR NAME      : KEYSYMBOL;
                                          VAR VALUE     : STRING;
                                          VAR LENGTH    : INTEGER   );

BEGIN (* GETIDENTIFIER *)

   WHILE NEXTCHAR.NAME IN [ LETTER, DIGIT ] DO

      STORENEXTCHAR( (* FROM *)       INPUTFILE,
                     (* UPDATING *)   LENGTH,
                                      CURRCHAR,
                                      NEXTCHAR,
                     (* IN *)         VALUE      );


   NAME := IDTYPE( (* OF *)     VALUE,
                   (* USING *)  LENGTH );

   IF NAME IN [ RECORDSYM, CASESYM, ENDSYM ]
      THEN
         CASE NAME OF

            RECORDSYM : RECORDSEEN := TRUE;

            CASESYM   : IF RECORDSEEN
                           THEN
                              NAME := CASEVARSYM;

            ENDSYM    : RECORDSEEN := FALSE

         END (* CASE *)

END; (* GETIDENTIFIER *)




PROCEDURE GETNUMBER( (* FROM *)       VAR INPUTFILE : TEXT;
                     (* UPDATING *)   VAR CURRCHAR,
                                          NEXTCHAR  : CHARINFO;
                     (* RETURNING *)  VAR NAME      : KEYSYMBOL;
                                      VAR VALUE     : STRING;
                                      VAR LENGTH    : INTEGER   );

BEGIN (* GETNUMBER *)

   WHILE NEXTCHAR.NAME = DIGIT DO

      STORENEXTCHAR( (* FROM *)       INPUTFILE,
                     (* UPDATING *)   LENGTH,
                                      CURRCHAR,
                                      NEXTCHAR,
                     (* IN *)         VALUE      );


   NAME := OTHERSYM

END; (* GETNUMBER *)
```

```
PROCEDURE GETCHARLITERAL( (* FROM *)            VAR INPUTFILE : TEXT;
                         (* UPDATING *)  VAR CURRCHAR,
                                             NEXTCHAR   : CHARINFO;
                         (* RETURNING *) VAR NAME       : KEYSYMBOL;
                                             VAR VALUE  : STRING;
                                             VAR LENGTH : INTEGER  );

BEGIN (* GETCHARLITERAL *)

   WHILE NEXTCHAR.NAME = QUOTE DO
      BEGIN

         STORENEXTCHAR( (* FROM *)      INPUTFILE,
                        (* UPDATING *) LENGTH,
                                       CURRCHAR,
                                       NEXTCHAR,
                        (* IN *)       VALUE    );

         WHILE NOT(NEXTCHAR.NAME IN [ QUOTE, ENDOFLINE, FILEMARK ]) DO

         STORENEXTCHAR( (* FROM *)      INPUTFILE,
                        (* UPDATING *) LENGTH,
                                       CURRCHAR,
                                       NEXTCHAR,
                        (* IN *)       VALUE    );


         IF NEXTCHAR.NAME = QUOTE
            THEN
               STORENEXTCHAR( (* FROM *)       INPUTFILE,
                              (* UPDATING *) LENGTH,
                                             CURRCHAR,
                                             NEXTCHAR,
                              (* IN *)       VALUE    )

      END;

   NAME := OTHERSYM

END; (* GETCHARLITERAL *)
```

```
FUNCTION CHARTYPE( (* OF *)              CURRCHAR,
                                         NEXTCHAR : CHARINFO )
                  (* RETURNING *)                                  : KEYSYMBOL;

VAR
    NEXTTWOCHARS: SPECIALCHAR;

    HIT: BOOLEAN;

    THISCHAR: KEYSYMBOL;


BEGIN (* CHARTYPE *)

    NEXTTWOCHARS[1] := CURRCHAR. VALUE;
    NEXTTWOCHARS[2] := NEXTCHAR. VALUE;

    THISCHAR := BECOMES;
    HIT      := FALSE;

    WHILE NOT(HIT OR (THISCHAR = CLOSECOMMENT)) DO
        IF NEXTTWOCHARS = DBLCHAR [THISCHAR]
            THEN
                HIT := TRUE
            ELSE
                THISCHAR := SUCC(THISCHAR);

    IF NOT HIT
        THEN
            BEGIN

                THISCHAR := SEMICOLON;

                WHILE NOT(HIT OR (PRED(THISCHAR) = PERIOD)) DO
                    IF CURRCHAR. VALUE = SQLCHAR [THISCHAR]
                        THEN
                            HIT := TRUE
                        ELSE
                            THISCHAR := SUCC(THISCHAR)

            END;

    IF HIT
        THEN
            CHARTYPE := THISCHAR
        ELSE
            CHARTYPE := OTHERSYM

END; (* CHARTYPE *)
```

```
PROCEDURE GETSPECIALCHAR( (* FROM *)        VAR INPUTFILE : TEXT;
                         (* UPDATING *)  VAR CURRCHAR,
                                             NEXTCHAR  : CHARINFO;
                         (* RETURNING *) VAR NAME      : KEYSYMBOL;
                                         VAR VALUE     : STRING;
                                         VAR LENGTH    : INTEGER   );

BEGIN (* GETSPECIALCHAR *)

   STORENEXTCHAR( (* FROM *)      INPUTFILE,
                 (* UPDATING *) LENGTH,
                                CURRCHAR,
                                NEXTCHAR,
                 (* IN *)       VALUE     );

   NAME := CHARTYPE( (* OF *) CURRCHAR,
                            NEXTCHAR );

   IF NAME IN DBLCHARS
     THEN

         STORENEXTCHAR( (* FROM *)      INPUTFILE,
                       (* UPDATING *) LENGTH,
                                      CURRCHAR,
                                      NEXTCHAR,
                       (* IN *)       VALUE        )

END; (* GETSPECIALCHAR *)
```

```
PROCEDURE GETNEXTSYMBOL( (* FROM *)      VAR INPUTFILE : TEXT;
                         (* UPDATING *)  VAR CURRCHAR,
                                             NEXTCHAR  : CHARINFO;
                         (* RETURNING *) VAR NAME      : KEYSYMBOL;
                                         VAR VALUE     : STRING;
                                         VAR LENGTH    : INTEGER   );

BEGIN (* GETNEXTSYMBOL *)

   CASE NEXTCHAR.NAME OF

      LETTER    : GETIDENTIFIER( (* FROM *)      INPUTFILE,
                                 (* UPDATING *)  CURRCHAR,
                                                 NEXTCHAR,
                                 (* RETURNING *) NAME,
                                                 VALUE,
                                                 LENGTH    );

      DIGIT     : GETNUMBER( (* FROM *)      INPUTFILE,
                             (* UPDATING *)  CURRCHAR,
                                             NEXTCHAR,
                             (* RETURNING *) NAME,
                                             VALUE,
                                             LENGTH    );

      QUOTE     : GETCHARLITERAL( (* FROM *)      INPUTFILE,
                                  (* UPDATING *)  CURRCHAR,
                                                  NEXTCHAR,
                                  (* RETURNING *) NAME,
                                                  VALUE,
                                                  LENGTH    );

      OTHERCHAR : BEGIN

                     GETSPECIALCHAR( (* FROM *)      INPUTFILE,
                                     (* UPDATING *)  CURRCHAR,
                                                     NEXTCHAR,
                                     (* RETURNING *) NAME,
                                                     VALUE,
                                                     LENGTH    );

                     IF NAME = OPENCOMMENT
                        THEN
                           GETCOMMENT( (* FROM *)     INPUTFILE,
                                       (* UPDATING *) CURRCHAR,
                                                      NEXTCHAR,
                                                      NAME,
                                                      VALUE,
                                                      LENGTH    )

                  END;

      FILEMARK  : NAME := ENDOFFILE

   END (* CASE *)

END; (* GETNEXTSYMBOL *)
```

```
PROCEDURE GETSYMBOL( (* FROM *)        VAR INPUTFILE : TEXT;
                     (* UPDATING *)  VAR NEXTSYM   : SYMBOLINFO;
                     (* RETURNING *) VAR CURRSYM   : SYMBOLINFO );

VAR
    DUMMY: SYMBOLINFO;


BEGIN (* GETSYMBOL *)

   DUMMY   := CURRSYM;
   CURRSYM := NEXTSYM;
   NEXTSYM := DUMMY  ;

   WITH NEXTSYM^ DO
      BEGIN

          SKIPSPACES( (* IN *)          INPUTFILE,
                      (* UPDATING *)  CURRCHAR,
                                      NEXTCHAR,
                      (* RETURNING *) SPACESBEFORE,
                                      CRSBEFORE      );

          LENGTH := 0;

          IF CURRSYM^.NAME = OPENCOMMENT
             THEN
                 GETCOMMENT( (* FROM *)        INPUTFILE,
                             (* UPDATING *)  CURRCHAR,
                                             NEXTCHAR,
                             (* RETURNING *) NAME,
                                             VALUE,
                                             LENGTH     )
             ELSE
                 GETNEXTSYMBOL( (* FROM *)        INPUTFILE,
                               (* UPDATING *)  CURRCHAR,
                                               NEXTCHAR,
                               (* RETURNING *) NAME,
                                               VALUE,
                                               LENGTH     )

      END (* WITH *)

END; (* GETSYMBOL *)
```

```
PROCEDURE INITIALIZE( (* RETURNING *)

                    VAR INPUTFILE,
                        OUTPUTFILE : TEXT;

                    VAR TOPOFSTACK  : INTEGER;

                    VAR CURRLINEPOS,
                        CURRMARGIN  : INTEGER;

                    VAR KEYWORD     : KEYWORDTABLE;

                    VAR DBLCHARS    : DBLCHRSET;

                    VAR DBLCHAR     : DBLCHARTABLE;

                    VAR SGLCHAR     : SGLCHARTABLE;

                    VAR RECORDSEEN  : BOOLEAN;

                    VAR CURRCHAR,
                        NEXTCHAR    : CHARINFO;

                    VAR CURRSYM,
                        NEXTSYM     : SYMBOLINFO;

                    VAR PPOPTION    : OPTIONTABLE    );
```

```
BEGIN (* INITIALIZE *)

   RESET(INPUTFILE);
   REWRITE(OUTPUTFILE);

   TOPOFSTACK   := 0;
   CURRLINEPOS  := 0;
   CURRMARGIN   := 0;


   KEYWORD [ PROGSYM    ] := 'PROGRAM   ' ;
   KEYWORD [ FUNCSYM    ] := 'FUNCTION  ' ;
   KEYWORD [ PROCSYM    ] := 'PROCEDURE ' ;
   KEYWORD [ LABELSYM   ] := 'LABEL     ' ;
   KEYWORD [ CONSTSYM   ] := 'CONST     ' ;
   KEYWORD [ TYPESYM    ] := 'TYPE      ' ;
   KEYWORD [ VARSYM     ] := 'VAR       ' ;
   KEYWORD [ BEGINSYM   ] := 'BEGIN     ' ;
   KEYWORD [ REPEATSYM  ] := 'REPEAT    ' ;
   KEYWORD [ RECORDSYM  ] := 'RECORD    ' ;
   KEYWORD [ CASESYM    ] := 'CASE      ' ;
   KEYWORD [ CASEVARSYM ] := 'CASE      ' ;
   KEYWORD [ OFSYM      ] := 'OF        ' ;
   KEYWORD [ FORSYM     ] := 'FOR       ' ;
   KEYWORD [ WHILESYM   ] := 'WHILE     ' ;
   KEYWORD [ WITHSYM    ] := 'WITH      ' ;
   KEYWORD [ DOSYM      ] := 'DO        ' ;
   KEYWORD [ IFSYM      ] := 'IF        ' ;
   KEYWORD [ THENSYM    ] := 'THEN      ' ;
   KEYWORD [ ELSESYM    ] := 'ELSE      ' ;
   KEYWORD [ ENDSYM     ] := 'END       ' ;
   KEYWORD [ UNTILSYM   ] := 'UNTIL     ' ;


   DBLCHARS := [ BECOMES, OPENCOMMENT ];

   DBLCHAR [ BECOMES     ] := ':=' ;
   DBLCHAR [ OPENCOMMENT ] := '(*' ;

   SGLCHAR [ SEMICOLON  ]  := ';' ;
   SGLCHAR [ COLON      ]  := ':' ;
   SGLCHAR [ EQUALS     ]  := '=' ;
   SGLCHAR [ OPENPAREN  ]  := '(' ;
   SGLCHAR [ CLOSEPAREN ]  := ')' ;
   SGLCHAR [ PERIOD     ]  := '.' ;

   RECORDSEEN := FALSE;


   GETCHAR( (* FROM *)       INPUTFILE,
            (* UPDATING *)   NEXTCHAR,
            (* RETURNING *)  CURRCHAR  );

   NEW(CURRSYM);
   NEW(NEXTSYM);

   GETSYMBOL( (* FROM *)      INPUTFILE,
              (* UPDATING *)  NEXTSYM,
              (* RETURNING *) CURRSYM  );
```

```
WITH PPOPTION [ PROGSYM ] DO
    BEGIN
        OPTIONSSELECTED    := [ BLANKLINEBEFORE,
                                SPACEAFTER ];
        DINDENTSYMBOLS     := [];
        GOBBLETERMINATORS  := []
    END;

WITH PPOPTION [ FUNCSYM ] DO
    BEGIN
        OPTIONSSELECTED    := [ BLANKLINEBEFORE,
                                DINDENTONKEYS,
                                SPACEAFTER ];
        DINDENTSYMBOLS     := [ LABELSYM,
                                CONSTSYM,
                                TYPESYM,
                                VARSYM ];
        GOBBLETERMINATORS  := []
    END;

WITH PPOPTION [ PROCSYM ] DO
    BEGIN
        OPTIONSSELECTED    := [ BLANKLINEBEFORE,
                                DINDENTONKEYS,
                                SPACEAFTER ];
        DINDENTSYMBOLS     := [ LABELSYM,
                                CONSTSYM,
                                TYPESYM,
                                VARSYM ];
        GOBBLETERMINATORS  := []
    END;

WITH PPOPTION [ LABELSYM ] DO
    BEGIN
        OPTIONSSELECTED    := [ BLANKLINEBEFORE,
                                SPACEAFTER,
                                INDENTTOCLP ];
        DINDENTSYMBOLS     := [];
        GOBBLETERMINATORS  := []
    END;

WITH PPOPTION [ CONSTSYM ] DO
    BEGIN
        OPTIONSSELECTED    := [ BLANKLINEBEFORE,
                                DINDENTONKEYS,
                                SPACEAFTER,
                                INDENTTOCLP ];
        DINDENTSYMBOLS     := [ LABELSYM ];
        GOBBLETERMINATORS  := []
    END;

WITH PPOPTION [ TYPESYM ] DO
    BEGIN
        OPTIONSSELECTED    := [ BLANKLINEBEFORE,
                                DINDENTONKEYS,
                                SPACEAFTER,
                                INDENTTOCLP ];
        DINDENTSYMBOLS     := [ LABELSYM,
                                CONSTSYM ];
        GOBBLETERMINATORS  := []
    END;
```

```
WITH PPOPTION [ VARSYM ] DO
   BEGIN
      OPTIONSSELECTED     := [ BLANKLINEBEFORE,
                               DINDENTONKEYS,
                               SPACEAFTER,
                               INDENTTOCLP ];
      DINDENTSYMBOLS      := [ LABELSYM,
                               CONSTSYM,
                               TYPESYM ];
      GOBBLETERMINATORS := []
   END;

WITH PPOPTION [ BEGINSYM ] DO
   BEGIN
      OPTIONSSELECTED     := [ DINDENTONKEYS,
                               INDENTBYTAB,
                               CRAFTER ];
      DINDENTSYMBOLS      := [ LABELSYM,
                               CONSTSYM,
                               TYPESYM,
                               VARSYM ];
      GOBBLETERMINATORS := []
   END;

WITH PPOPTION [ REPEATSYM ] DO
   BEGIN
      OPTIONSSELECTED     := [ INDENTBYTAB,
                               CRAFTER ];
      DINDENTSYMBOLS    := [];
      GOBBLETERMINATORS := []
   END;

WITH PPOPTION [ RECORDSYM ] DO
   BEGIN
      OPTIONSSELECTED     := [ INDENTBYTAB,
                               CRAFTER ];
      DINDENTSYMBOLS    := [];
      GOBBLETERMINATORS := []
   END;

WITH PPOPTION [ CASESYM ] DO
   BEGIN
      OPTIONSSELECTED     := [ SPACEAFTER,
                               INDENTBYTAB,
                               GOBBLESYMBOLS,
                               CRAFTER ];
      DINDENTSYMBOLS    := [];
      GOBBLETERMINATORS := [ OFSYM ]
   END;

WITH PPOPTION [ CASEVARSYM ] DO
   BEGIN
      OPTIONSSELECTED     := [ SPACEAFTER,
                               INDENTBYTAB,
                               GOBBLESYMBOLS,
                               CRAFTER ];
      DINDENTSYMBOLS    := [];
      GOBBLETERMINATORS := [ OFSYM ]
   END;
```

```
WITH PPOPTION [ OFSYM ] DO
   BEGIN
      OPTIONSSELECTED     := [ CRSUPPRESS,
                               SPACEBEFORE ];
      DINDENTSYMBOLS      := [];
      GOBBLETERMINATORS := []
   END;

WITH PPOPTION [ FORSYM ] DO
   BEGIN
      OPTIONSSELECTED     := [ SPACEAFTER,
                               INDENTBYTAB,
                               GOBBLESYMBOLS,
                               CRAFTER ];
      DINDENTSYMBOLS      := [];
      GOBBLETERMINATORS := [ DOSYM ]
   END;

WITH PPOPTION [ WHILESYM ] DO
   BEGIN
      OPTIONSSELECTED     := [ SPACEAFTER,
                               INDENTBYTAB,
                               GOBBLESYMBOLS,
                               CRAFTER ];
      DINDENTSYMBOLS      := [];
      GOBBLETERMINATORS := [ DOSYM ]
   END;

WITH PPOPTION [ WITHSYM ] DO
   BEGIN
      OPTIONSSELECTED     := [ SPACEAFTER,
                               INDENTBYTAB,
                               GOBBLESYMBOLS,
                               CRAFTER ];
      DINDENTSYMBOLS      := [];
      GOBBLETERMINATORS := [ DOSYM ]
   END;

WITH PPOPTION [ DOSYM ] DO
   BEGIN
      OPTIONSSELECTED     := [ CRSUPPRESS,
                               SPACEBEFORE ];
      DINDENTSYMBOLS      := [];
      GOBBLETERMINATORS := []
   END;

WITH PPOPTION [ IFSYM ] DO
   BEGIN
      OPTIONSSELECTED     := [ SPACEAFTER,
                               INDENTBYTAB,
                               GOBBLESYMBOLS,
                               CRAFTER ];
      DINDENTSYMBOLS      := [];
      GOBBLETERMINATORS := [ THENSYM ]
   END;
```

```
WITH PPOPTION [ THENSYM ] DO
    BEGIN
        OPTIONSSELECTED    := [ INDENTBYTAB,
                                CRAFTER ];
        DINDENTSYMBOLS    := [];
        GOBBLETERMINATORS := []
    END;

WITH PPOPTION [ ELSESYM ] DO



    BEGIN
        OPTIONSSELECTED    := [ CRBEFORE,
                                DINDENTONKEYS,
                                DINDENT,
                                INDENTBYTAB,
                                CRAFTER ];
        DINDENTSYMBOLS    := [ IFSYM,
                                ELSESYM ];
        GOBBLETERMINATORS := []
    END;

WITH PPOPTION [ ENDSYM ] DO
    BEGIN
        OPTIONSSELECTED    := [ CRBEFORE,
                                DINDENTONKEYS,
                                DINDENT,
                                CRAFTER ];
        DINDENTSYMBOLS    := [ IFSYM,
                                THENSYM,
                                ELSESYM,
                                FORSYM,
                                WHILESYM,
                                WITHSYM,
                                CASEVARSYM,
                                COLON,
                                EQUALS ];
        GOBBLETERMINATORS := []
    END;

WITH PPOPTION [ UNTILSYM ] DO
    BEGIN
        OPTIONSSELECTED    := [ CRBEFORE,
                                DINDENTONKEYS,
                                DINDENT,
                                SPACEAFTER,
                                GOBBLESYMBOLS,
                                CRAFTER ];
        DINDENTSYMBOLS     := [ IFSYM,
                                THENSYM,
                                ELSESYM,
                                FORSYM,
                                WHILESYM,
                                WITHSYM,
                                COLON,
                                EQUALS ];
        GOBBLETERMINATORS := [ ENDSYM,
                                UNTILSYM,
                                ELSESYM,
                                SEMICOLON ];
    END;
```

```
WITH PPOPTION [ BECOMES ] DO
    BEGIN
        OPTIONSSELECTED    := [ SPACEBEFORE,
                                SPACEAFTER,
                                GOBBLESYMBOLS ];
        DINDENTSYMBOLS     := [];
        GOBBLETERMINATORS := [ ENDSYM,
                                UNTILSYM,
                                ELSESYM,
                                SEMICOLON ]
    END;


WITH PPOPTION [ OPENCOMMENT ] DO
    BEGIN
        OPTIONSSELECTED    := [ CRSUPPRESS ];
        DINDENTSYMBOLS     := [];
        GOBBLETERMINATORS := []
    END;

WITH PPOPTION [ CLOSECOMMENT ] DO
    BEGIN
        OPTIONSSELECTED    := [ CRSUPPRESS ];
        DINDENTSYMBOLS     := [];
        GOBBLETERMINATORS := []
    END;

WITH PPOPTION [ SEMICOLON ] DO
    BEGIN
        OPTIONSSELECTED    := [ CRSUPPRESS,
                                DINDENTONKEYS,
                                CRAFTER ];
        DINDENTSYMBOLS     := [ IFSYM,
                                THENSYM,
                                ELSESYM,
                                FORSYM,
                                WHILESYM,
                                WITHSYM,
                                COLON,
                                EQUALS ];
        GOBBLETERMINATORS := []
    END;

WITH PPOPTION [ COLON ] DO
    BEGIN
        OPTIONSSELECTED    := [ SPACEAFTER,
                                INDENTTOCLP ];
        DINDENTSYMBOLS     := [];
        GOBBLETERMINATORS := []
    END;
```

```
WITH PPOPTION [ EQUALS ] DO
   BEGIN
      OPTIONSSELECTED   := [ SPACEBEFORE,
                             SPACEAFTER,
                             INDENTTOCLP ];
      DINDENTSYMBOLS    := [];
      GOBBLETERMINATORS := []
   END;

WITH PPOPTION [ OPENPAREN ] DO
   BEGIN
      OPTIONSSELECTED   := [ GOBBLESYMBOLS ];
      DINDENTSYMBOLS    := [];
      GOBBLETERMINATORS := [ CLOSEPAREN ]
   END;

WITH PPOPTION [ CLOSEPAREN ] DO
   BEGIN
      OPTIONSSELECTED   := [];
      DINDENTSYMBOLS    := [];
      GOBBLETERMINATORS := []
   END;

WITH PPOPTION [ PERIOD ] DO
   BEGIN


      OPTIONSSELECTED   := [ CRSUPPRESS ];
      DINDENTSYMBOLS    := [];
      GOBBLETERMINATORS := []
   END;

WITH PPOPTION [ ENDOFFILE ] DO
   BEGIN
      OPTIONSSELECTED   := [];
      DINDENTSYMBOLS    := [];
      GOBBLETERMINATORS := []
   END;

WITH PPOPTION [ OTHERSYM ] DO
   BEGIN
      OPTIONSSELECTED   := [];
      DINDENTSYMBOLS    := [];
      GOBBLETERMINATORS := []
   END


END; (* INITIALIZE *)
```

```
FUNCTION STACKEMPTY (* RETURNING *) : BOOLEAN;

BEGIN (* STACKEMPTY *)

   IF TOP = 0
      THEN
         STACKEMPTY := TRUE
      ELSE
         STACKEMPTY := FALSE

END; (* STACKEMPTY *)


FUNCTION STACKFULL (* RETURNING *) : BOOLEAN;

BEGIN (* STACKFULL *)

   IF TOP = MAXSTACKSIZE
      THEN
         STACKFULL := TRUE
      ELSE
         STACKFULL := FALSE

END; (* STACKFULL *)
```

```
PROCEDURE POPSTACK( (* RETURNING *) VAR INDENTSYMBOL : KEYSYMBOL;
                                    VAR PREVMARGIN   : INTEGER   );

BEGIN (* POPSTACK *)

   IF NOT STACKEMPTY
      THEN
         BEGIN

            INDENTSYMBOL := STACK[TOP].INDENTSYMBOL;
            PREVMARGIN   := STACK[TOP].PREVMARGIN;

            TOP := TOP - 1

         END

      ELSE
         BEGIN
            INDENTSYMBOL := OTHERSYM;
            PREVMARGIN   := 0
         END

END; (* POPSTACK *)




PROCEDURE PUSHSTACK( (* USING *) INDENTSYMBOL : KEYSYMBOL;
                                 PREVMARGIN   : INTEGER   );

BEGIN (* PUSHSTACK *)

   TOP := TOP + 1;

   STACK[TOP].INDENTSYMBOL := INDENTSYMBOL;
   STACK[TOP].PREVMARGIN   := PREVMARGIN

END; (* PUSHSTACK *)
```

```
PROCEDURE WRITECRS( (* USING *)         ·         NUMBEROFCRS : INTEGER;
                    (* UPDATING *)     VAR CURRLINEPOS : INTEGER;
                    (* WRITING TO *) VAR OUTPUTFILE   : TEXT     );

VAR
    I: INTEGER;


BEGIN (* WRITECRS *)

   IF NUMBEROFCRS > 0
      THEN
         BEGIN

            FOR I := 1 TO NUMBEROFCRS DO
               WRITELN(OUTPUTFILE);

            CURRLINEPOS := 0

         END

END; (* WRITECRS *)




PROCEDURE INSERTCR( (* UPDATING *)    VAR CURRSYM    : SYMBOLINFO;
                    (* WRITING TO *) VAR OUTPUTFILE : TEXT          );

CONST
      ONCE = 1;


BEGIN (* INSERTCR *)

   IF CURRSYM^. CRSBEFORE = 0
      THEN
         BEGIN

            WRITECRS( ONCE, (* UPDATING *)    CURRLINEPOS,
                            (* WRITING TO *) OUTPUTFILE  );

            CURRSYM^. SPACESBEFORE := 0

         END

END; (* INSERTCR *)
```

```
PROCEDURE INSERTBLANKLINE( (* UPDATING *)    VAR CURRSYM : SYMBOLINFO;
                           (* WRITING TO *) VAR OUTPUTFILE : TEXT   );

CONST
     ONCE  = 1;
     TWICE = 2;


BEGIN (* INSERTBLANKLINE *)

   IF CURRSYM^. CRSBEFORE = 0
      THEN
         BEGIN

            IF CURRLINEPOS = 0
               THEN
                  WRITECRS( ONCE, (* UPDATING *)   CURRLINEPOS,
                                  (* WRITING TO *) OUTPUTFILE   )
               ELSE
                  WRITECRS( TWICE, (* UPDATING *)   CURRLINEPOS,
                                   (* WRITING TO *) OUTPUTFILE   );

            CURRSYM^. SPACESBEFORE := 0

         END

      ELSE
         IF CURRSYM^. CRSBEFORE = 1
            THEN
               IF CURRLINEPOS > 0
                  THEN
                     WRITECRS( ONCE, (* UPDATING *)   CURRLINEPOS,
                                     (* WRITING TO *) OUTPUTFILE   )

END; (* INSERTBLANKLINE *)
```

```
PROCEDURE LSHIFTON( (* USING *) DINDENTSYMBOLS : KEYSYMSET );

VAR
    INDENTSYMBOL: KEYSYMBOL;
    PREVMARGIN  : INTEGER;


BEGIN (* LSHIFTON *)

   IF NOT STACKEMPTY
      THEN
         BEGIN

            REPEAT

               POPSTACK( (* RETURNING *) INDENTSYMBOL,
                                         PREVMARGIN   );

                  IF INDENTSYMBOL IN DINDENTSYMBOLS
                     THEN
                        CURRMARGIN := PREVMARGIN

               UNTIL NOT(INDENTSYMBOL IN DINDENTSYMBOLS)
                     OR (STACKEMPTY);

               IF NOT(INDENTSYMBOL IN DINDENTSYMBOLS)
                  THEN
                     PUSHSTACK( (* USING *) INDENTSYMBOL,
                                            PREVMARGIN   )

         END

END; (* LSHIFTON *)




PROCEDURE LSHIFT;

VAR
    INDENTSYMBOL: KEYSYMBOL;
    PREVMARGIN  : INTEGER;


BEGIN (* LSHIFT *)

   IF NOT STACKEMPTY
      THEN
         BEGIN
            POPSTACK( (* RETURNING *) INDENTSYMBOL,
                                      PREVMARGIN   );
            CURRMARGIN := PREVMARGIN
         END

END; (* LSHIFT *)
```

```
PROCEDURE INSERTSPACE( (* USING *)         VAR SYMBOL     : SYMBOLINFO;
                       (* WRITING TO *) VAR OUTPUTFILE : TEXT        );

BEGIN (* INSERTSPACE *)

   IF CURRLINEPOS < MAXLINESIZE
      THEN
         BEGIN

            WRITE(OUTPUTFILE, SPACE);

            CURRLINEPOS := CURRLINEPOS + 1;

            WITH SYMBOL^ DO
               IF (CRSBEFORE = 0) AND (SPACESBEFORE > 0)
                  THEN
                     SPACESBEFORE := SPACESBEFORE - 1

         END

END; (* INSERTSPACE *)




PROCEDURE MOVELINEPOS( (* TO *)         NEWLINEPOS  : INTEGER;
                       (* FROM *) VAR CURRLINEPOS : INTEGER;
                       (* IN *)   VAR OUTPUTFILE  : TEXT    );

VAR
   I: INTEGER;

BEGIN (* MOVELINEPOS *)

   FOR I := CURRLINEPOS+1 TO NEWLINEPOS DO
      WRITE(OUTPUTFILE, SPACE);

   CURRLINEPOS := NEWLINEPOS

END; (* MOVELINEPOS *)
```

```
PROCEDURE PRINTSYMBOL( (* IN *)                    CURRSYM      : SYMBOLINFO;
                       (* UPDATING *)  VAR CURRLINEPOS : INTEGER;
                       (* WRITING TO *) VAR OUTPUTFILE  : TEXT        );

VAR
   I: INTEGER;


BEGIN (* PRINTSYMBOL *)

   WITH CURRSYM^ DO
      BEGIN

         FOR I := 1 TO LENGTH DO
            WRITE(OUTPUTFILE, VALUE[I]);

         CURRLINEPOS := CURRLINEPOS + LENGTH

      END (* WITH *)

END; (* PRINTSYMBOL *)
```

```
PROCEDURE PPSYMBOL( (* IN *)                    CURRSYM    : SYMBOLINFO;
                   (* WRITING TO *) VAR OUTPUTFILE : TEXT        );

CONST
     ONCE = 1;

VAR
    NEWLINEPOS: INTEGER;


BEGIN (* PPSYMBOL *)

   WITH CURRSYM^ DO
      BEGIN

         WRITECRS( (* USING *)        CRSBEFORE,
                   (* UPDATING *)     CURRLINEPOS,
                   (* WRITING TO *)   OUTPUTFILE  );

         IF (CURRLINEPOS + SPACESBEFORE > CURRMARGIN)
            OR (NAME IN [ OPENCOMMENT, CLOSECOMMENT ])
            THEN
               NEWLINEPOS := CURRLINEPOS + SPACESBEFORE
            ELSE
               NEWLINEPOS := CURRMARGIN;

         IF NEWLINEPOS + LENGTH > MAXLINESIZE
            THEN
               BEGIN

                  WRITECRS( ONCE, (* UPDATING *)   CURRLINEPOS,
                                  (* WRITING TO *) OUTPUTFILE  );

                  IF CURRMARGIN + LENGTH <= MAXLINESIZE
                     THEN
                        NEWLINEPOS := CURRMARGIN
                     ELSE
                        IF LENGTH < MAXLINESIZE
                           THEN
                              NEWLINEPOS := MAXLINESIZE - LENGTH
                           ELSE
                              NEWLINEPOS := 0

               END;

         MOVELINEPOS( (* TO *)      NEWLINEPOS,
                      (* FROM *)    CURRLINEPOS,
                      (* IN *)      OUTPUTFILE  );

         PRINTSYMBOL( (* IN *)          CURRSYM,
                      (* UPDATING *)    CURRLINEPOS,
                      (* WRITING TO *)  OUTPUTFILE  )

      END (* WITH *)

END; (* PPSYMBOL *)
```

```
PROCEDURE RSHIFTTOCLP( (* USING *) CURRSYM : KEYSYMBOL );
   FORWARD;

PROCEDURE GOBBLE( (* SYMBOLS FROM *) VAR INPUTFILE    : TEXT;
                  (* UP TO *)            TERMINATORS : KEYSYMSET;
                  (* UPDATING *)     VAR CURRSYM,
                                         NEXTSYM     : SYMBOLINFO;
                  (* WRITING TO *)   VAR OUTPUTFILE  : TEXT        );

BEGIN (* GOBBLE *)

   RSHIFTTOCLP( (* USING *) CURRSYM^.NAME );

   WHILE NOT(NEXTSYM^.NAME IN (TERMINATORS + [ENDOFFILE])) DO
      BEGIN

         GETSYMBOL( (* FROM *)      INPUTFILE,
                    (* UPDATING *)  NEXTSYM,
                    (* RETURNING *) CURRSYM   );

         PPSYMBOL( (* IN *)         CURRSYM,
                   (* WRITING TO *) OUTPUTFILE )

      END; (* WHILE *)

   LSHIFT

END; (* GOBBLE *)
```

```
PROCEDURE RSHIFT( (* USING *) CURRSYM : KEYSYMBOL );

BEGIN (* RSHIFT *)

    IF NOT STACKFULL
       THEN
           PUSHSTACK( (* USING *) CURRSYM,
                                  CURRMARGIN);

    IF CURRMARGIN < SLOWFAIL1
       THEN
           CURRMARGIN := CURRMARGIN + INDENT1
       ELSE
           IF CURRMARGIN < SLOWFAIL2
              THEN
                  CURRMARGIN := CURRMARGIN + INDENT2

END; (* RSHIFT *)



PROCEDURE RSHIFTTOCLP;

BEGIN (* RSHIFTTOCLP *)

    IF NOT STACKFULL
       THEN
           PUSHSTACK( (* USING *) CURRSYM,
                                  CURRMARGIN);

    CURRMARGIN := CURRLINEPOS

END; (* RSHIFTTOCLP *)
```

```
BEGIN (* PRETTYPRINT *)

    INITIALIZE( INPUTFILE,   OUTPUTFILE, TOP,        CURRLINEPOS,
                CURRMARGIN, KEYWORD,    DBLCHARS,   DBLCHAR,
                SQLCHAR,    RECORDSEEN, CURRCHAR,   NEXTCHAR,
                CURRSYM,    NEXTSYM,    PPOPTION );

    CRPENDING := FALSE;

    WHILE (NEXTSYM^.NAME <> ENDOFFILE) DO
        BEGIN

            GETSYMBOL( (* FROM *)       INPUTFILE,
                       (* UPDATING *)  NEXTSYM,
                       (* RETURNING *) CURRSYM   );

            WITH PPOPTION [CURRSYM^.NAME] DO
                BEGIN

                    IF (CRPENDING AND NOT(CRSUPPRESS IN OPTIONSSELECTED))
                        OR (CRBEFORE IN OPTIONSSELECTED)
                            THEN
                                BEGIN
                                    INSERTCR( (* USING *)     CURRSYM,
                                              (* WRITING TO *) OUTPUTFILE );
                                    CRPENDING := FALSE
                                END;

                    IF BLANKLINEBEFORE IN OPTIONSSELECTED
                        THEN
                            BEGIN
                                INSERTBLANKLINE( (* USING *)     CURRSYM,
                                                 (* WRITING TO *) OUTPUTFILE );
                                CRPENDING := FALSE
                            END;

                    IF DINDENTONKEYS IN OPTIONSSELECTED
                        THEN
                            LSHIFTON(DINDENTSYMBOLS);

                    IF DINDENT IN OPTIONSSELECTED
                        THEN
                            LSHIFT;

                    IF SPACEBEFORE IN OPTIONSSELECTED
                        THEN
                            INSERTSPACE( (* USING *)     CURRSYM,
                                         (* WRITING TO *) OUTPUTFILE );

                    PPSYMBOL( (* IN *)       CURRSYM,
                              (* WRITING TO *) OUTPUTFILE );
```

```
            IF SPACEAFTER IN OPTIONSSELECTED
            THEN
                INSERTSPACE( (* USING *)        NEXTSYM,
                             (* WRITING TO *) OUTPUTFILE );

            IF INDENTBYTAB IN OPTIONSSELECTED
            THEN
                RSHIFT( (* USING *) CURRSYM^. NAME );




            IF INDENTTOCLP IN OPTIONSSELECTED
            THEN
                RSHIFTTOCLP( (* USING *) CURRSYM^. NAME );

            IF GOBBLESYMBOLS IN OPTIONSSELECTED
            THEN
                GOBBLE( (* SYMBOLS FROM *) INPUTFILE,
                        (* UP TO *)        GOBBLETERMINATORS,
                        (* UPDATING *)     CURRSYM,
                                           NEXTSYM,
                        (* WRITING TO *)   OUTPUTFILE        );

            IF CRAFTER IN OPTIONSSELECTED
            THEN
                CRPENDING := TRUE

        END (* WITH *)

    END; (* WHILE *)

IF CRPENDING
THEN
    WRITELN(OUTPUTFILE)

END.
```

BIBLIOGRAPHY

[A1] Armstrong, Russel M., *Modular Programming in COBOL,* John Wiley and Sons, New York, 1973.

[B1] Baker, F. T., Chief Programmer Team Management of Production Programming, *IBM Systems Journal,* Vol. 11, No. 1, 1972.

[C1] Cave, William C., *A Method for Management Control of Software Development,* CENTACS Software Report, No. 41, U.S. Army Electronics Division, Fort Monmouth, N.J., 1974.

[C2] Chmura, Louis J., and Ledgard, Henry F., *COBOL with Style,* Hayden Publishing Company, Rochelle Park, N.J., 1976.

[C3] Cooper, Laura, and Smith, Marilyn, *Standard FORTRAN: A Problem Solving Approach,* Houghton Mifflin, Boston, 1973.

[C4] Cougar, J. Daniel, Evolution of Business System Analysis Techniques, *Computing Surveys,* Vol. 5, No. 3, Sept. 1973.

[D1] Dahl, O. J., Dijkstra, E. W., and Hoare, C. A. R., *Structured Programming,* Academic Press, New York, 1972.

[D2] Dijkstra, Edsgar W., Goto Statement Considered Harmful, *Communications of the ACM,* Vol. 11, No. 3, March 1968.

[D3] Dijkstra, Edsgar W., The Humble Programmer, 1972 Turing Award Lecture, *Communications of the ACM,* Vol. 15, No. 10, Oct. 1972.

[G1] Goldstine, H. H., and von Neumann, J., Planning and Coding for an Electronic Computing Instrument—Part II, Volume 1, *John von Neumann—Collected Works,* Vol. 5, Pergamon Press, New York, 1963.

[J1] Jensen, Kathleen, and Wirth, Nicklaus, *PASCAL User Manual and Report,* Springer-Verlag, New York, Heidelberg, and Berlin, 1975.

[K1] Kernighan, Brian, and Plauger, William, *The Elements of Programming Style,* McGraw-Hill, New York, 1973.

[K2] Kreitzberg, Charles B., and Schneiderman, Ben, *The Elements of FORTRAN Style: Techniques for Effective Programming,* Harcourt Brace Jovanovich, New York, 1972.

[L1] Ledgard, Henry F., *Programming Proverbs,* Hayden Books, Rochelle Park, N.J., 1975.

[L2] Ledgard, Henry F., *Programming Proverbs for FORTRAN Programmers,* Hayden Books, Rochelle Park, N.J., 1975.

[L3]   Ledgard, Henry F, and Cave, William, "COBOL Under Control," *Communications of the ACM*, Nov. 1976.

[L4]   Ledgard, Henry F., and Marcotty, Michael, "A Genealogy of Control Structures," *Communications of the ACM*, Nov. 1975.

[M1]   McCracken, Daniel D., *A Guide to FORTRAN IV Programming*, John Wiley and Sons, New York, 1972.

[M2]   Mills, Harlan B., *Mathematical Foundations for Structured Programs*, Technical Report, FSC 72-6012, IBM Federal Systems Division, Gaithersburg, Md., 1972.

[S1]   Spier, Michael J., *The Typset-10 Codex Programmaticus*, Technical Report, Digital Equipment Corporation, 1974.

[S2]   Strachey, Christopher, "Systems Analysis and Programming," in *Readings from Scientific American*, W.H. Freeman and Co., San Francisco, 1971.

[S3]   Strunk, William, Jr., and White, E. B., *The Elements of Style*, Macmillan, New York, 1959.

[V1]   Van Tassel, Donnie, *Program Style, Design, Efficiency, Debugging, and Testing*, Prentice-Hall, Englewood Cliffs, N.J., 1974.

[W1]   Weinberg, Gerald M., *The Psychology of Computer Programming*, Van Nostrand Reinhold, New York, 1971.

[W2]   Wirth, Niklaus, "Program Development by Stepwise Refinement," *Communications of the ACM*, Vol. 14, No. 4., April 1971.

[Y1]   Yourdon, E., *Techniques of Program Structure and Design*, Prentice-Hall, Englewood Cliffs, N.J., 1975.

[Z1]   _____, American Standard FORTRAN, USA Standards Institute, 1966.

[Z2]   _____, *FORTRAN IV Language*, IBM System/360 and System C28-6515-8, 1971.

[Z3]   _____, Proposed ANS FORTRAN Standard, American National Standards Committee, 1977.

INDEX

INDEX